Everything a MOM should know about her YOUNG CHILD

Gloriana Montero

e625.com

EVERYTHING A MOM SHOULD KNOW ABOUT HER YOUNG CHILD
e625 - 2025
Dallas, Texas

Translated by: **Sophia Leys**
Edited by: **Sarah Hauge**
Interior design and cover adaptation: **Bárbara Soriano**

ISBN: 9781954149762

PRINTED IN THE UNITED STATES

Table of Contents

Gratitude

To my daughter, Victoria, who since the womb has taught me that the true meaning of living is giving to others, who has brought me to my knees, and who has revealed many aspects of myself that I never knew before. I'm so grateful to God for giving me the privilege of being your mom! Thank you for making my days bright!

To my husband, Danilo, who has always affirmed me as a mother. Thank you for your confidence in me and making me feel secure. Thank you for supporting me while I wrote this book. And thank you that, in addition to all the marvelous things you are, you are a good cook.

To my mother, Gloria, who has always been an inspiration to me. Thank you for always being there when I need you. Thank you for teaching me wisdom, for infecting me with your spirit of faith and joy, and, over all else, for molding me with your love.

To every mom who is also a friend because they have given me their advice. Thank you to all those women I admire. I hope to see in my children what I see in theirs. Great job! Not only will these moms' children rise up to praise them, but there is an entire society that urgently needs them.

To my loving Lord, who gives me strength in times of weakness, wisdom in dark times, and faith that He will do His purpose in me and in mine. Thank you that I can truly rely on you.

The love of a mother is a treasure that lasts forever and leaves an unremovable mark in our lives.

Prologue
By Danilo Montero

On December 23, 2010, at 1:14 a.m., our lives changed forever with the arrival of Victoria. We had finished the course on natural birth the night before, and as a form of celebration, I prepared Gloriana a hot bath with bath salts, not knowing that could induce labor. The next day, I woke up to find my wife feeling sick and feverish. After many hours in the hospital, the doctor came into the room to inform us that they would have to remove our daughter in her eighth month. I can still remember what I was thinking and feeling while I watched them prepare my wife. The moment had come!

In a matter of minutes they placed my newly-born daughter in my arms. Gloriana, still sedated, asked me how she looked, and I, crazed in happiness, told her she was beautiful.

We were introduced to parenthood, just like that. That day, Gloriana began the everlasting job of discovering what being a mother means, and how that reality is lived day by day.

Learning to take care of a fragile new baby is only the beginning. They first open their eyes only a short time after birth. From that moment on we keep our own eyes wide open to discover who we're holding in our laps.

In becoming a parent, suddenly you understand more about yourself as a son or daughter, as part of a family, your previous life experiences, and your beliefs. You witness this all begin in the new person before you. Although sometimes parents compare a child to moldable clay that, like potters, we have to "shape," we cannot help but be amazed at the reality that this "clay" already has its own qualities and preferences, temperament, and other traits that are innate parts of themself.

My mother-in-law explained it this way: Being a parent means molding our children without breaking them. We should learn to give them shape according to what we consider good, right, and, most

importantly, what is glorifying to God. And at the same time, we must respect the essence of the being God had entrusted to us.

I have been able to witness much of Gloriana's journey through motherhood firsthand. Gloriana embodies that balance of profound love for her daughter, the strength and clarity of a leader, and the unquenchable thirst of a student devoted to the subject of motherhood. She is always asking questions and seeking ways of doing it better. Gloriana has committed herself 100% to the role of mother. This role comes with indescribable challenges, with many successes and mistakes along the way.

This book is full of the ideas and lessons learned in Gloriana's journey as a mother, focused on children from ages 0 to 12. There are many important aspects of motherhood addressed in these pages. This book goes far beyond focusing on discipline, delving into God's devotion and teaching about principles and values, identity and sexuality.

I'm confident that in this book you will find resources to help you develop in the noble task of motherhood in a way that honors God and leads to abundant fruit in the lives of your children.

Danilo

Introduction

Experiencing the miracle of pregnancy and the birth of a baby is perhaps the greatest privilege the Lord has given to women. Motherhood intersects with us at a moment in time and changes us forever. We are never the same.

Someone once said, "Children are the cause of the greatest joys, but also the greatest sorrows." A mother's heart dreams of seeing her children fulfilled and thriving. She desires this so much that she is willing to sacrifice her own dreams for theirs. She knows that even if they no longer live in her womb, they will live forever in her heart.

Am I doing it right? This is a question we mothers constantly ask ourselves. Our doubts and questions are important because they help us review what we are doing and why, to decide what we want to try or change, and to search for real and effective information on how to do our job better.

The task of shaping our children's lives in a holistic, solid, and healthy way is nuanced. Just as we strive to select the best among many food options and offer our kids a balanced diet, so too do we, as mothers, navigate the supermarket of life, choosing between endless options to determine what we believe is necessary and beneficial for our children's development.

When it comes to physical development, we can lean on the support and guidance of doctors who regularly measure and monitor our children's healthy growth. But who helps us measure their growth in emotions, identity, and character? Who tells us about healthy standards in these areas? What if we only realize something is wrong when it becomes evident in a behavior down the road—something we might have avoided if we had intervened earlier?

Faced with all these questions and driven by the desire to share with other mothers some of the things I have learned throughout this beautiful yet challenging journey of motherhood, the idea of writing this book was born. I am grateful to Dr. Lucas Leys and his initiative, 625, for trusting that I could contribute something to the vision of shaping this generation between the ages of 6 and 25.

My contribution, in reality, is indirect. This book is for mothers, who are the most important shapers of the new generation: those who nurture, embrace, and educate children and adolescents every day.

The time to lay the foundations that will sustain our children's lives is in their first 10 years. This is the stage during which the body, psyche, and heart are being formed and are still moldable. It is also the time when children see their parents as the number one reference in their lives. When they reach adolescence, this changes. That is why our work as mothers throughout our children's first 520 weeks must be focused and intentional. This is the period of greatest influence we will have in our child's entire life, and it's an opportunity that will never occur again.

I hope this book provides you with tools you can implement in your life and in your child's life. In these pages you will find information on how to help your child be more secure in the person God designed them to be, develop a healthy sexuality, shape their character as a person of God, establish firm faith, and understand the purpose of discipline, among other topics. All of this, of course, is framed within the principles of God's Word.

I encourage you to walk with Jesus as you journey through this enormous responsibility of motherhood. He promises to give you rest and to send the Holy Spirit to help you, whatever your need may be. May the hope of knowing that in this precious and challenging journey, you are not alone fill you with strength—because He is always with you!

Chapter 01

HAPPY MOM, HAPPY HOME

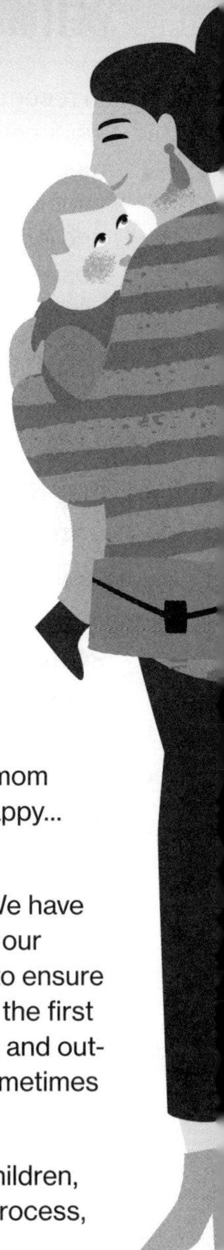

"Your children will be like vigorous olive shoots around your table. That is the blessing of the Lord for those who fear Him."
Psalm 128:3-4

A few years ago, I heard a funny but very true saying: "If mom is happy, everyone in the house is happy. If mom is not happy... everyone better hide!"

Mothers are often referred to as the heart of the home. We have been given the ability to care for the overall well-being of our family members. We strive to keep the family united and to ensure that each member grows in a balanced way. Mothers are the first to wake up and the last to go to bed; we work both inside and outside the home; we eat last—often while standing—and sometimes even skip meals.

A mother's heart is sacrificial. She gives herself for her children, for her home, and often doesn't even realize that, in the process, she is sacrificing herself.

SETTING PRIORITIES

In recent decades, women have gained power and respect in work environments that demand great dedication and commitment. This has brought many benefits in terms of personal and financial growth but has also put many mothers between a rock and a hard place, especially when work gets in the way of their desire to spend more time with their children.

Faced with this reality, we must learn to make decisions that bring a healthy balance to our lives. Seeking wisdom in this is essential because while some tasks can be easily delegated, in your child's heart, no one can replace you. No one else can do what only you can.

"By dedicating yourself to your children, you are investing in something that no one can ever take away from you or from them!"

"By dedicating yourself to your children, you are investing in something that no one can ever take away from you or from them!"

One of the biggest lies many women believe is this:

"Dedicating myself to my children is a waste of time. With my skills and talents, I could be doing something more productive."

No! Quite the opposite! By dedicating yourself to your children, you are investing in something that no one can ever take away from you or from them!

I really liked a comment from the well-known pastor and counselor Wayne Cordeiro in his book *Running on Empty*. He pointed out that when it comes to setting priorities, our guide should be this:

"We must face what only we can accomplish."

Brian Dyson, former COO of Coca-Cola, gave a graduation speech at Georgia Tech in 1996, in which he used an analogy to explain how to distinguish what is most important in life:

"Imagine life as a game in which you are juggling some five balls in the air. You name them – work, family, health, friends and spirit – and you're keeping all of these in the air. You will soon understand that work is a rubber ball. If you drop it, it will bounce back. But the other four balls – family, health, friends and spirit – are made of glass. If you drop one of these, they will be irrevocably scuffed, marked, nicked, damaged, or even shattered. They will never be the same. You must understand that and strive for balance in your life."

God's vision for both men and women is that we prosper in everything, just as our soul prospers... but not at the cost of our soul! To achieve this balance, we need great wisdom to make the right decisions, adjusting along the way so that our lives and homes flourish as described in Psalm 128.

IT'S A MATTER OF TIME

Our window of opportunity to influence our children's lives is essentially limited to their first 10 years. From birth to age 10, children form their strongest bonds, establish their identity, develop self-esteem, discover their strengths, shape their character, and build habits that will define whether they become successful in the future—or not.

Knowing this, we must be very intentional, ensuring that we meet our children's physical and mental, emotional, and spiritual needs, guiding them toward a healthy, well-rounded development.

GET READY!

Before starting a trip on a plane, the flight attendants always explain to the passengers what the safety procedures are in case of an emergency. One of the possible emergencies on airplanes is a depressurization of the cabin. This happens when the air pumping system stops working. At more than 10,000 feet of altitude, every person needs additional oxygen; therefore, if the main air pumping system fails, special masks will drop over each passenger to provide them with the necessary oxygen.

The safety instructions aim, then, to prepare us. By becoming aware of the possible events, we are no longer "foolish or senseless" people, but instead we prepare ourselves to face them. Knowledge is key for times of crisis.

What has always caught my attention is that in all airlines, the instruction for mothers is the same: "Put your own mask on first, and then put it on the children." It seems counterintuitive, right? However, this instruction reveals a great truth: If you, as a mom, are doing well, then you will be able to help the little ones, and not the other way around!

Before becoming moms, all women have certain ideals about how we are going to carry out this beautiful task. We dream of holding our babies in our arms, of breastfeeding them, dressing them with ribbons, bows and little ties... but the truth is that we barely think about the big challenges that are inherent to motherhood (maybe we even ignore them still!), like the exhaustion you feel after a whole month without sleeping enough, or the pain and wounds from breastfeeding, or the acid reflux, or the tantrums, the falls, the hospital visits, the illnesses, etc., etc.!

He promises to be with us every day, the good ones and the bad!

It is true that, just as every pregnancy is unique, so is every birth and every growth process. However, I have noticed a generalized attitude among Christians of rejecting or denying that complications might exist. Of course, I'm not saying we shouldn't pray asking for everything to go the best way. But it is mistaken to believe that just because we are Christians, we will never have any problem or complication. What is true is that in the midst of any problem or challenge the Lord will say to us: "Do not fear, I am with you." He promises to be with us every day, the good ones and the bad!

But the truth is that in life, just like on a plane, the more informed we are, the more we can prepare. That's why there is literature that somehow "trains" you for the task. For me, books about pregnancy and the first months of the baby were of great help. They helped me understand what was normal and what wasn't during that time.

So yes, it is possible that we may have complications during labor, that we may suffer from postpartum depression, that our children may be born with certain health problems or with a syndrome... But in the face of any situation or diagnosis, the truth is that we are not alone, and that we are more than conquerors because the One who is by our side is much greater than us and than any situation we may go through.

Shortly before having our daughter Victoria, I was very close to a friend who was expecting her first child. She, even though she was married to an anesthesiologist, said that she was not going to ask for the epidural because she believed that Christ had carried all her pains on the cross, including labor pains. In the United States, it is necessary to ask for this anesthesia before labor, to schedule the doctor and the medical team. If you don't schedule it in advance, it's possible that it may take a long time for the doctor to arrive when you need them. My friend's husband was living the peak of being an anesthesiologist! However, with much love, he warned her that natural childbirth was something very painful, and he recommended having the anesthesia ready, just in case. But she stayed firm in her belief... until the big day came. When the contractions began to get more and more painful, she was screaming for the anesthesia... but since she hadn't requested it in advance, by the time the anesthesiologist on duty arrived, she was already so dilated that they couldn't administer it. When I went to visit her after giving birth, the first thing she said to me was: "Glory, when it's your turn, don't even think of not asking for the anesthesia!"

I have also heard women, even pastors, tell me how terrible it was to suffer from postpartum depression. Some only cried and felt a great sadness that lasted for several months. Others couldn't hold their babies for almost a month, except to feed them. Others spent time in a corner of their bed, not even wanting to shower. But the saddest part was hearing that several of them were judged by people in the church "because it wasn't possible for a Christian woman to go through that." How terrible! I think that maybe the main cause of this bad attitude is ignorance, because not everyone knows that postpartum depression has its origin in a physical condition. When the baby is no longer inside, the body goes through a stage of hormonal adjustment, and that's why many times it is necessary to ask a doctor for help to regulate our body as soon as possible.

As I said before, we cannot guarantee that everything will go the way we expect. But we should be prepared, and surround ourselves with wise and capable people for any situation that we do not know how to face. People who support us, and who encourage us to get through the hard days in the best way possible.

I remember that before giving birth to Victoria, a friend told me that the first few months were going to be very hard, and that the exhaustion was going to be extreme. But the good news she gave me was that they passed quickly! She told me: "Just hold on through the first three months. You'll see that once the baby turns three months old, everything is going to get better." And that's exactly what happened! You can't imagine how her words echoed in my mind during the hard moments. Every time I felt exhausted, I would tell myself: "This stage will pass soon. Almost there." And that gave me strength for one more day.

ASK FOR HELP

What a blessing it was to have my mom at home during Victoria's first months! And to have the full support and commitment of my husband! It made me love him even more deeply. Together they made my journey much easier.

So my advice is: Seek all the support you can! Not everyone can be as available as my husband and mother were for me, but there are many ways to offer practical support, like having groceries delivered, or stopping by to clean your kitchen. All of these small acts are needed and deeply appreciated!

LET GO OF UNNECESSARY BURDENS

Studies have shown that while babies are in our womb, they are affected by the emotions we, the mothers, experience. For example, a friend in Honduras told me how she almost gave birth to her baby at 6 months pregnant when she found out her husband had been kidnapped, because her emotions affected her pregnancy. But this is also true for less "dramatic" emotions. Babies feel, inside their mother's belly, everything she is feeling. Even after birth, while we are breastfeeding, it is not only what we eat that is transmitted through the milk to the babies, but also what we feel. They are the first ones to receive from us our joys or sorrows, our peace or our bitterness.

Moms nourish not only the body of our children,but also their souls.

"Mothers nourish not only their children's bodies but also their souls."

And the truth is that moms nourish not only the body of our children, but also their souls. That is why your emotional health is vital for the emotional health of your little ones!

We all have a story that shapes us. Although we are born with free hands, emotionally healthy, and with an attitude to explore everything and try everything, as we grow we start to change... We acquire fears from unpleasant experiences. We adopt concepts about ourselves and others that are not necessarily true. And we interpret life's challenges in certain ways because maybe we were not equipped with basic emotional skills to face life.

It is sad to hear people acknowledge that what they once promised not to do when they had children is exactly what they are doing now that they have them! Rejection, abandonment, anger, impatience... Why? Because, without realizing it, we allow the past to interfere with our present.

Building a family is not easy. Living together and the dynamics of married life come with their own challenges, which add extra burdens. And if we face that with our own baggage of jealousy, insecurities, resentment, and aggressiveness... then that home is no longer a place of peace, and sooner or later our family will become a battlefield where there will be other victims besides mom and dad.

The burdens turn into weapons, and then we strike because we've been struck, we hurt because it's our defense, and we seek personal satisfaction at all costs, even if that means harming ourselves and, worse, those we love the most. Without meaning to, we "make them pay" for things that happened many years ago to our closest loved ones.

Think about it. What happens when we carry excess baggage in our lives? I observe at least three consequences:

- **Someone has to pay for the excess baggage.** Who is going to do it? Usually, those who are close to us, just like on every trip...

- **It causes emotional exhaustion.** The burdens end up creating a fog that clouds the reality of things. I've heard many women say that, because of their emotional and physical exhaustion, they end up questioning whether all the effort is worth it, whether the sacrifice is worth it, whether it's worth continuing to try... Emotional exhaustion is dangerous because it makes us vulnerable to getting hurt and making poor decisions. It takes away our drive to pay attention to the details, to fight every day to make things better. It changes the loving and affirming words that only we can give our children and our husband into complaints, grumbling, and offenses.

- **It affects our health**. Did you know that the leading cause of death in women is heart problems? Poor stress management, constant anger, or simply neglecting your own health because you're always tending to other things–these can all trigger heart problems, stomach issues, and many more.

Moreover, we must remember that we can't give others what we don't have. So, moms, it's a good moment to let go of everything we've been carrying for years and allow ourselves to be filled with what we long to give. How do we do that? It's simple: hand over the baggage to the One who already paid for it. The only one who has asked to carry our burdens is Jesus Christ. He himself said:

"Come to me, all you who are weary and burdened, and I will give you rest. Take my yoke upon you and learn from me, for I am gentle and humble in heart, and you will find rest for your souls. For my yoke is easy and my burden is light." (Matthew 11:28–30, NIV)

No matter how good the anti-stress techniques or other methods we use to try to feel better are, they will eventually be temporary solutions because we're not truly dealing with the root of the problem in our soul. On the other hand, notice that the yoke Jesus invites us to carry includes certain things:

- The yoke makes you walk with someone. The yoke is what ties work animals to a plow, and what keeps them walking together to double the strength. Jesus doesn't confront us alone–He meets us in our way of life and lets us make a decision: either we continue alone carrying everything we have, or we join Him! United to Jesus, our work becomes much lighter!

- The yoke requires adjustments. When a young ox was being trained to plow, it would be yoked with an older, experienced ox. If the young one wanted to go its own way, it couldn't–because it was tied to the experienced ox who led it where to go. Jesus said: "Let me teach you, because I am humble and gentle at heart." Walking with Jesus equips us better for any task we must take on!

Jesus wants to walk with you in this arduous but beautiful task of being a mother.

Remember that humility is the ability to understand that He is everything to us, and that we submit to His guidance. He may tell you to let go of that resentment that's been bothering you for years, to forgive, or even to go and speak with certain people from your past, and break the yoke with them. Jesus will teach you to love people—even if they don't deserve it. There is no greater freedom than that. The truth is, now you walk with someone who makes life lighter!

When we walk with Jesus, our view of others changes too. We begin to see people the way He sees them. We notice their wounds and brokenness, which leads us to be merciful and treat them differently. Also, when Jesus gives us rest for our souls, we can embrace our little ones, and discipline and teach them with love, not harshness.

And when you feel tired, remember: do not accept substitutes. When God is not our place of refuge, other things we try to replace Him with will cause imbalance in our lives. Some of the refuges women seek are tranquilizers, extreme exercise, new relationships, etc. But what we really need is to come again and again to Him, who is the source of life, so we can drink what our soul needs: the freedom of God's forgiveness, the truth of His acceptance, and the inheritance we have as daughters of God.

Jesus wants to walk with you in this arduous but beautiful task of being a mother. He wants you to raise children with tender and humble hearts. Healthy children who also know how to live life walking with Him. And don't forget that to do this, your children need a healthy mom—physically, mentally, and emotionally—so that you can guide and love them in a healthy way.

Set your priorities. Get ready. Ask for help. Let go of unnecessary burdens. Walk yoked with Jesus. And remember that "happy mom, happy home!"

Chapter 02

UNDERSTANDING THE STAGES OF DEVELOPMENT

Knowledge, along with the skill with which we apply that knowledge, is the key to success in any task or challenge we face. As mothers, when we understand the stage our little one is going through and what they need for healthy development at that stage, we can:

- Apply the knowledge we are acquiring to skillfully manage the physical, emotional, and cognitive needs of our child.
- Gain a better perspective on the time we have to achieve desirable objectives and move on to the next stage.
- Prepare ourselves with cameras and videos to capture moments that will never happen again.
- We enjoy each stage more. (And we can reassure ourselves in challenging times that no matter what, it's just a stage and won't last forever!)

In this chapter, I will provide a general overview of the different stages our children go through, highlighting the key aspects of each. Later, in the following chapters, I will go into more detail about specific topics that should be addressed differently in each stage. So, let's begin!

STAGE: ZERO TO ONE YEAR

"I Need You NOW!"

This is the stage when...

- **No one can sleep.**
  And that's why there are so many books on the market offering advice on how to establish routines so that your baby sleeps a little more than two hours at night... for mom's mental health and everyone else's at home!

- **Moms have never smelled worse.**
  During the baby's first few months, the newborn's constant demands force moms to take lightning-fast showers. Oh, how we miss those times when we could take long showers and do our hair!

- **You've never been needed this much.**
  This is a 24/7 job, especially if you're breastfeeding. I remember that sometimes my husband, Danilo, would be holding our baby. When I walked by, it seemed like she was looking at a cow, exclusively there to serve her. She would immediately lick her lips and stretch out her little arms for me to pick her up and nurse her.

DEVELOPMENT DURING THIS STAGE

PHYSICAL DEVELOPMENT	VERBAL DEVELOPMENT
3-4 months: They lift their head and chest	**0-6 weeks:** Different cries and vowel sounds.
4-6 months: They reach for objects with their hands and can roll over.	**3 months:** They turn their head when they hear your voice and make consonant sounds.
6-8 months: They sit up and grasp objects with two fingers.	**6 months:** They imitate your voice and babble.
6-10 months: They crawl; some start walking	**9 months:** They understand simple words.
11-12 months: They stand up with help; some begin to walk.	**12 months:** They understand about 70 words and say their first words.
MENTAL DEVELOPMENT	**EMOTIONAL DEVELOPMENT**
They explore the world through their five senses.	**6 weeks:** They give their first social smile.
They begin to be more aware of everything happening around them.	**2 months:** They like looking at themselves in the mirror.
	4 months: They distinguish happy and sad faces.
	7 months: They show surprise in response to loud noises.

DON'T FORGET:

- Establish routines and follow them. This will help you meet your body's needs, such as sleep, movement, rest, food, etc., and will also keep your baby happy.
- Create a home environment filled with praise and worship. Take time to sing, pray for your child, and, most importantly, create a peaceful environment around your baby.
- Take advantage of all the help you can get with secondary household chores!

STAGE: ONE TO TWO YEARS

"I do it myself."

This is the stage when...

- **Nothing goes as planned.**
  Anything can happen, and the day rarely goes as planned. Maybe you finally have the whole family in the car ready to go, when suddenly the baby soils their diaper (and sometimes, their clothes too). You have to start the whole process again–go back inside, change them, and return them to the car seat.
- **No clean shoulders.**
  Babies at this age tend to use our clothes–especially our shoulders–to clean their mouths, noses, and hands.
- **The baby can do everything "on their own."**
  The baby is no longer a baby. This is when their journey toward independence begins. These little ones will insist on doing things by themselves.

  The biggest challenge at this stage is their constant "I can do it!" and all that entails. Frustration when trying to put on their shoes alone, danger when attempting to climb up and down stairs alone, and tantrums when they want to dress, eat, and do everything by themselves.

Physical and mental changes happen at this stage more than at any other. Your little one can already express themselves better, they can walk, and now they're ready to reach everything, try everything, and conquer everything! However, life for them is quite hard. Everything they want to do requires learning a new skill—holding a cup, using the toilet...

The best part is their positive attitude toward challenges. The great thing is that they are discovering their potential!

For moms, this is perhaps the most physically exhausting stage. Keeping up with a constantly moving, high-energy child will take a lot out of you. You may even have to put away your high heels for a while because you'll need to be ready at any moment to jump up and run to rescue them.

THEIR DEVELOPMENT DURING THIS STAGE

PHYSICAL DEVELOPMENT	VERBAL DEVELOPMENT
12-15 months: They sit, crawl, and walk.	**18 months:** They point at objects when you name them.
15-18 months: They can walk backward and sideways.	**18 months:** They say 10 to 20 words, mostly nouns and pronouns.
18-24 months: They go up and down stairs and jump in place.	**24 months:** They say 40 to 50 words and form two-word sentences.

24-36 months: They throw a ball overhead, stand on one foot for a moment, and some show hand dominance.

36 months: They say 300 to 400 words (though some may be hard to understand).

MENTAL DEVELOPMENT	EMOTIONAL DEVELOPMENT
Follow simple instructions.	Enjoy role-playing activities.
Benefit from repetition.	Struggle to share and experience separation anxiety.
Do not understand others' perspectives.	May start biting, screaming, and throwing tantrums.
Confuse past, present, and future.	Play alongside others but don't yet know how to play with them.
Learn through music, movement, and art.	Recognize basic emotions in others.

DON'T FORGET:

- Encourage your child to have confidence in themselves: "Yes, you can do it!"
- Be firm with "NO," but don't yell. Keep a calm tone of voice so your little one knows their limits and who is in control.
- Be flexible, but with order. For example, define play areas for your child's well-being and safety.

- Make sure pets are safe and that your child is safe around them.
- Establish spiritual principles and teach your child about God through simple statements. For example, "God created you," "God loves you," and "He is always with you."
- Enjoy worship time with your child. Dance together. Celebrate the Lord!
- Read to your child every night. A love for reading starts early!

STAGE: THREE TO FOUR YEARS

"Why?"

This is the stage when...

- **Everything can be imagined.**
  At this age, a child's imagination is their reality. She is a princess or a doctor. He is a pirate or a superhero. This imagination feels so real that it can also bring fear, so we must be cautious. Stories about monsters seem real to them.
- **The "Why?" questions never end.**
  Children's curiosity at this age is unlimited, and they never stop asking questions. Keep in mind that four-year-olds often ask "Why" not just to understand *why* something happens, but also *how* it happens. So when they ask "Why?" for the third or fourth time, don't get frustrated. It's not that they don't understand you, they just want more information to make sense of their world.

THEIR DEVELOPMENT DURING THIS STAGE

PHYSICAL DEVELOPMENT	VERBAL DEVELOPMENT
They balance on one foot for 5 to 10 seconds.	It becomes easier to understand them.
They cut with scissors.	They may struggle with some sounds like r, l, s, j, ch.
They ride a tricycle.	They say more than 1,000 words (but really, who's counting?).
They climb stairs on alternating feet.	They answer questions like What? Where? When?
They button and unbutton their clothes.	

MENTAL DEVELOPMENT	EMOTIONAL DEVELOPMENT
They begin to distinguish between real and unreal.	At age three, they may bite, scream, and throw tantrums.
They may struggle to tell the difference between truth and lies.	They enjoy humor and simple jokes.
They still don't understand others' perspectives.	They can express basic emotions when asked.

MENTAL DEVELOPMENT	EMOTIONAL DEVELOPMENT
They live in the present; their memory of past events is limited.	They can say what makes them happy or sad
They learn by categorizing things simply.	They may have nightmares about specific fears (fire, darkness, monsters).
They start identifying cause-and-effect relationships.	They respond well to stories as a way of discussing emotions.

DON'T FORGET:

- Before disciplining your child, remember that their life is still very confusing, and rules may not always make sense to them.
- They may struggle to understand why certain things are acceptable and others aren't. For example, it can be hard for them to understand why throwing a ball is okay but throwing a rock isn't, or why hugging Dad tightly is fine but not a newborn baby.
- Set limits. At this stage, help your child develop self-control. Statements like "If you yell, I won't give it to you" or "If you throw a tantrum, you won't get it" calmly express boundaries.
- Establish routines for bathtime, meals, and playtime. This gives them stability and security.
- Listen to your child. Their questions about God may surprise you, but remember that faith in an unseen God may not seem clear or obvious to a young child. (Later, you'll find a whole chapter on this topic!)

KINDERGARTEN AND FIRST GRADE STAGE

"Mommy, look!"

This is the stage when...

- **They say things that you'll remember forever.**

  Your little one enters the school routine, and even though dropping them off at school may bring some tears, their unfiltered words will make you laugh.

  It's a great idea to keep a record of their first nonsensical phrases or their special way of saying things. My friend Fiona Mellet, a mother of five, once told me that with her youngest child, she didn't rush to correct his speech. She knew that, as the youngest, she would never experience these moments again, so why hurry?

  Her child would say "cabause" instead of "because." A person outside the home corrected him: "It's 'because'!" But Fiona quickly replied, "NO! 'Cabause' is fine!"

- **It takes effort to keep up with school schedules and demands.**

  The school routine is a big challenge for both kids and parents. Getting children used to alarms telling them when to wake up, dealing with sleepy little bears who refuse to get ready, getting them dressed, brushing their hair, feeding them breakfast, and trying to get them to school on time – it's not easy!

  For kids who didn't attend daycare as toddlers, adjusting to school can be hard. They go from being the center of attention at home to just one among many children in a classroom.

THEIR DEVELOPMENT DURING THIS STAGE

PHYSICAL DEVELOPMENT	SOCIAL DEVELOPMENT
They can brush their teeth, wash and dry their hands, and use the toilet independently.	They want to please and help others.
Ages six to eight: They lose their baby teeth	They switch quickly between activities and groups.
They draw people with full bodies.	They struggle to ask for help.
They write their name.	They need help learning to take turns and to lose gracefully.
They learn to tie their shoes.	They show little preference for gender when choosing playmates.
They need 10-12 hours of sleep each night.	

MENTAL DEVELOPMENT	EMOTIONAL DEVELOPMENT
They can focus on an activity for five to 15 minutes.	They can show extreme emotions
They begin to understand ironic humor and tell simple jokes.	They express emotions more through play and art than words.

They recognize and can name numbers, shapes, and colors	They tend to be optimistic.
They understand the difference between need and want, as well as real and imaginary.	They need to face moderate challenges and experience succes
They still don't logically interpret cause and effect.	They are very sensitive to harsh criticism, tone of voice, and body language.

DON'T FORGET:

- Help your child learn by giving them concrete examples of principles and behaviors you want them to follow.
- Play at their level. A child at this age feels highly motivated when you get involved and show interest in their games.
- Accompany them in learning. This is the stage when they learn to read and write, which can be a big challenge. Show patience and consistency until you're sure they are making progress.
- Deepen their understanding of God's principles. Teach them that they can trust God in any situation, help them understand the Golden Rule (treat others as you want to be treated), and guide them in making good decisions.

STAGE: SECOND AND THIRD GRADE

"Everything has to be fair"

This is the stage when...

- **What's "fair" matters a lot.**

  Children at this age develop a stronger awareness of what justice means and will often judge your actions as "not fair." They may argue with siblings and classmates about fairness and report any perceived injustices committed by teachers, siblings, etc. Detective and police games, as well as superhero vs. villain play, are especially appealing to them at this stage.

- **They notice their differences.**

  Kids start becoming more aware of their individuality. Depending on the situation, this can bring them satisfaction or embarrassment. As mothers, we must be attentive and instill virtues like humility ("What matters is not being the best, but giving your best") and help them with their self-esteem when they feel they're not good enough in a certain area (since everyone has strengths and weaknesses).

- **Fun abounds.**

  This is one of the best stages of childhood. If you spend time with your child, their enthusiasm, energy, and funny antics will allow you to enjoy them immensely.

THEIR DEVELOPMENT DURING THIS STAGE

PHYSICAL DEVELOPMENT	SOCIAL DEVELOPMENT
They are more independent when bathing.	They enjoy cooperating and participating in group activities.
They continue losing baby teeth, including molars.	They highly value fairness and consistency.
They grow rapidly in height and weight (girls tend to grow faster than boys).	They may struggle with highly competitive situations.
They improve hand-eye coordination.	They begin to prefer playmates of their own gender.
They play more, tire more quickly, and still need 10-11 hours of sleep each night.	They need time to talk and process their daily experiences.
MENTAL DEVELOPMENT	**EMOTIONAL DEVELOPMENT**
They can focus on an activity for up to 30 minutes.	They are better at controlling their emotions.
They understand cause and effect.	They may still confuse "I feel..." with "I am..."
They recognize patterns and symbols.	They are easily embarrassed by failures.
Their concept of time is still limited.	They generally feel more independent and secure.
They learn well through hands-on activities, problem-solving, codes, and puzzles.	They develop a sense of humor through riddles, magic tricks, and jokes.

DON'T FORGET:

- Encourage your child to develop a healthy self-concept and self-esteem. This stage lays the foundation for their identity.
- Use their interest in justice and differences as an opportunity to highlight diversity and how we all need each other, no matter how different we are.
- Take advantage of available resources (such as children's books) to teach them about teamwork and the unique skills of each person.
- Avoid giving them, or allowing others to give them, nicknames based on their weaknesses.

STAGE: FOURTH AND FIFTH GRADE

"I know that; I can do that."

This is the stage when...

- **Friends matter more.**

  What their friends approve or disapprove of becomes highly significant. If you notice changes in the way your child dresses or talks, look at their friends. Best friends become everything. And, sorry to say, their friends' opinions will matter more than yours—at least for the next 10 years!

- **Games are about competition, not just fun.**

  Their self-confidence makes them feel unstoppable. They are always ready to compete because they want others to recognize their strengths and abilities.

- **Their confidence guides them.**

  They are no longer the youngest in elementary school and feel ready to move into a stage of greater independence. Parents must help them build healthy confidence in themselves. They need to know we believe in their potential and trust them. We need confident children to succeed in the next phase of school life!

THEIR DEVELOPMENT DURING THIS STAGE

PHYSICAL DEVELOPMENT	SOCIAL DEVELOPMENT
They may show early signs of puberty: acne, mood swings, and changes in height and weight (girls between ages 8-11, boys between ages 9-12).	They value their friends' approval and often challenge authority.
They continue losing baby molars	They seek more privacy.
They improve in speed, strength, and body control.	They may excel in competitive situations.
They need physical activity and may seem restless.	They benefit from having a best friend of the same gender.

They still require 10-11 hours of sleep each night.	They may develop romantic interests (such as having a crush) and experience physical affection.
MENTAL DEVELOPMENT	**EMOTIONAL DEVELOPMENT**
They can focus on an activity for up to 45 minutes.	They may feel self-conscious about their bodies.
They transition from learning to read to reading to learn.	They enjoy word games and sarcasm, but their humor can become negative.
They can collaborate and understand rules and consequences.	They need to experience some failure to understand the consequences of their actions.
They recognize perspectives different from their own.	They still hold onto family values and beliefs but may start asking challenging questions.
They still struggle with abstract concepts.	They want to be seen as independent and mature.

DON'T FORGET:

- Give your child challenges that match their abilities—things they can accomplish and situations where they can succeed.
- Help your child build healthy friendships. Everyone needs friends! Get to know the kids they spend time with, and encourage friendships outside of school that bring positive influences. Teach them the value of true friendship and how to be a good friend.

- Be a good friend to your child by showing interest in what they like.
- Help them grow in wisdom, faith, and their relationship with God.

As I said at the beginning of this chapter, each stage is just that—a stage. The good and the bad, the easy and the difficult—it will all pass. Enjoy it as much as you can!

Chapter 03

PERFECTLY CREATED

“I knew you even before I formed you in your mother’s womb.” Jeremiah 1:5

During the early years of life, the foundations of a human being are formed. During this time the basis of identity is established, allowing a child to answer the question “Who am I?” with confidence. This answer goes beyond just a name, surname, or biological sex: It encompasses a set of defining factors such as personality, character, ethnicity, faith, and more. These characteristics make each individual UNIQUE and DIFFERENT from others.

Although identity is not static, it is anchored in a stable foundation that shapes its most characteristic traits. This foundation is laid during childhood and adolescence.

One of our most important responsibilities as parents is to consciously work on shaping a healthy identity in our children. Identity is not something they are born with—it is constructed and redefined, mainly during the early years of life and primarily within the home. It is at home where they will either develop a sense of security or insecurity that will accompany them for the rest of their lives. It is there that they will learn to love themselves, as they will be accepted just as they are. They will also learn to love others. Just as we strive to teach our children to embrace their uniqueness, we must also teach them to respect others for theirs. We will encourage good qualities and correct both their thought processes and inappropriate actions, guiding them toward the development of a healthy identity.

Identity influences every aspect of our lives. The healthier our identity is:

- The more opportunities we will have to build enriching relationships.
- The more creative we will be in our work.
- The better prepared we will be to face adversity.
- The more inclined we will be to treat others with respect.
- The more we will experience the joy of living!

Developing a healthy identity also helps us build a proper self-concept and a strong self-esteem.

Self-concept is the image a person has of themselves. It includes everything a person knows about themselves regarding their abilities, physical traits, knowledge, unique characteristics, and more.

Self-concept can become distorted when:

- A child is made to believe that having certain physical features or skin color makes them "inferior" or not "beautiful."
- They are not affirmed in what they do well, nor encouraged to try new things.
- They are not taught how to overcome failures, which leads them to think: "I'm not good at this."

Self-esteem is connected to how a person feels about what they know about themselves. We want every human being to be able to answer "yes" to this! Self-esteem is the emotional result of self-concept. It serves as the foundation for emotions, so it's very important that our self-esteem is healthy!

Self-esteem also develops in a child as a result of their experiences and interactions with others. It is shaped by "what others say about me" and begins in childhood with an unspoken question children wonder of their parents: "Do they like me just as I am?"

As parents, we must ensure that we provide our children with positive answers to this question and avoid words or situations that might harm their sense of self. But even more importantly, we must teach them the true source of their identity. We need to show them what God says about them in His Word. Otherwise, throughout life they will continue to question their worth and base their self-love on the judgment of others.

HOW DO CHILDREN DEVELOP THEIR IDENTITY?

This is a natural process that begins at birth. The first question they seek to answer is, "Who am I in relation to others?" Through the voices and scents of those around them, babies begin to distinguish between people. Generally, they will first recognize their mother's scent and their father's voice. During this stage, attachment plays a crucial role in identity formation.

After a few months, babies also begin to recognize certain "strangers"—those who are close to them who are not their parents. They will become experts at noticing similarities and differences between the people around them. As a result of these interactions, babies learn to feel valued and protected.

Around three years of age, children start to recognize more about people's appearances and their many variations. In more racially homogeneous communities, young children may express surprise when they encounter people with skin tones or physical features different from what they are accustomed to.

As a result of these interactions, babies learn to feel valued and protected.

Since we live in Houston, my husband and I made sure our daughter interacted with people from diverse racial and cultural backgrounds from an early age. Her preschool teacher was a beautiful young woman of Korean descent. After her first day of school, our daughter Victoria came home and said: "Mommy, my teacher's eyes are almost closed, but she can still see me–right through the center!" In the same classroom, she had an African-American classmate and another classmate from Pakistan. She was the only Hispanic child in the group. From a young age, she was immersed in diversity, which helped her understand that human beings are externally different. We emphasized to her that while we may look different on the outside, we all have the same value before God and others.

By the time children reach school age, they are much more aware of their differences, and they start to care about what others think of them. It is natural for them to begin comparing themselves based on physical traits, discussing whether they find themselves attractive, or–if they are from a different ethnic background–feeling embarrassed about speaking their native language in front of other children. In short, they may feel uncomfortable being different.

Nick Vujicic shares in his book *Life Without Limits* how, at the age of eight, he attempted suicide after realizing he was different from everyone else. Due to a genetic condition called tetra-amelia syndrome, he was born without arms and legs, with only two small, underdeveloped feet. Thanks to the support of his parents and his faith in God, he was able to overcome his struggles. He accepted that, despite his limitations, God had a plan for his life and wanted to use him for a greater purpose. Embracing this, he completed his university studies at the age of 21, founded multiple businesses, and even acted in a movie, winning awards for his performance. Today, he works as a motivational speaker, inspiring people around the world. He is married to a wonderful woman, and together they have four children.

HOW TO BUILD A HEALTHY IDENTITY?

The identity I want my children to develop is rooted in what their Creator says about them. Therefore, I must be intentional in reminding them of this truth—not just so they remember it, but so they internalize it and make it their own.

Take advantage of every moment—whether dressing them, bathing them, brushing their hair in front of the mirror, or walking with them to school—to speak to them about who they are, using God's Word. I love repeating to my daughter what Psalm 139:

The identity I want my children to develop is rooted in what their Creator says about them.

"Lord, you have examined my heart and you know me well. You know when I sit down and when I rise up. Even from afar, you understand my thoughts. You trace my path before me and tell me where to rest. You know where I am every moment. You know what I am going to say before I even say it, Lord. You surround me on all sides and place your hand upon my head.

Such wonderful knowledge is beyond my understanding; it is so great that I cannot comprehend it. I can never escape from your Spirit! I can never flee from your presence!" (Verses 1-7)

"You made all the delicate inner parts of my body and knit me together in my mother's womb. Thank you for making me so wonderfully complex! Your workmanship is marvelous—how well I know it. You watched me as I was being formed in secret. Your eyes saw my unformed body; every day of my life was recorded in your book. Every moment was laid out before a single day had passed.

How precious are your thoughts about me, O God! They cannot be numbered! I cannot count them; they outnumber the grains of sand! And when I wake up, you are still with me." (Verses 13-18)

WE MUST CONSTANTLY CORRECT THE THOUGHTS WE HAVE ABOUT HOW WE SEE OURSELVES.

With this Psalm, I like to emphasize the following to my daughter:

- God loves you so much that He always wants to be with you. Even when some people choose to leave, He will always stay. Even when Mom or Dad are not around, He will be there.

- There is no way to escape His presence. You will never be alone!

- If you need help or feel sad, you can talk to Him. Prayer connects you directly to heaven. He wants to hear you–to know what you think and feel. He will also speak to your heart, reminding you of His truth about who you are.

- You are beautiful because you were designed by God. A perfect creation–inside and out! It's not just about the color of your eyes or whether your hair is curly or straight. It's about all the gifts and talents He placed within you, waiting for you to discover and enjoy.

- God wants you to live life to the fullest, doing what you love and shining brightly to illuminate this world with His love!

Remember that the search for a healthy identity lasts a lifetime. As adults, we too must constantly correct the thoughts we have about how we see ourselves–thoughts that pull us away from who we truly are. I admire the attitude of Pastor Joel Osteen, the senior pastor of the church where we work and serve. He says that every day, when he looks in the mirror, he greets himself as a beloved child of the Almighty God–capable, anointed, focused, and handsome. But what do we say to ourselves in the mirror? "Oh, you look terrible!", "You're such a mess–no wonder no one values you!" And who knows how many other negative things?

Isn't the world already hostile enough? Why add to it by bombarding yourself with these kinds of thoughts?

Take control of your mind. Draw close to God's Word every day so you can discover what the Almighty says about you—and take ownership of it! This is not about feeling superior to others. It's about living with the right mindset—the one we need to face life with confidence.

When we think and speak well of ourselves, we will naturally do the same for our children. Instead of speaking negatively about them, we will be attentive when we hear them whispering self-doubting thoughts. We will remind them that they are a gift from God and encourage them to see themselves that way.

OTHER PRACTICAL TIPS TO HELP DEVELOP A HEALTHY IDENTITY AND SELF-ESTEEM IN YOUR CHILD:

- Love him for who he is. Remind him of his strengths, his abilities, and the qualities that make him unique and special.
- Tell her you believe in her. This will give her confidence in herself.
- Help him manage frustration when he makes mistakes.
- Remind her that practice makes perfect. It's okay to be wrong—she just needs to try again.
- Don't overprotect him. Give him the chance to experience both defeats and victories, and celebrate his successes.
- Our goal should not be to change her or turn her into our ideal child, but to help her become successful by developing within God's design, with the unique potential and characteristics He has given her.

- Never, ever compare him to his siblings or other children.
- Do not pass judgment on him or label him with phrases like "You're a mess," "You're not good at that," or "You always do things wrong."

Those words will be ingrained in his mind for the rest of his life and will affect him more than you can imagine.

DISCOVERING OUR CHILDREN

Just as we do not choose the physical characteristics of our children, we also do not choose their abilities, tastes, and personality. But unlike physical traits, this genetic information is not as obvious, and it takes time for our children to begin showing their talents, such as being good at sports, music, or mathematics. Also, as they grow, they will begin to show their personal tastes and preferences for certain areas in particular. It is fascinating to watch them develop and see everything that God has placed in them begin to emerge!

In this, our main responsibility as mothers is to create an environment where they can grow healthy. In the Bible, we find the case of a family with two sons. They were twins, and just as they were very different from each other physically, they were also different in their tastes and personality. Esau was hairy and loved adventure (I imagine him sweaty all the time) and dedicated himself to hunting animals. His brother Jacob was the opposite: he was hairless, and I don't know why I imagine him much slimmer than Esau, and he preferred to stay at home tending the sheep, that is, a different type of activity. The Bible mentions that Esau was the father's favorite, and Jacob was the mother's favorite. This, as we all know, led to a series of events with sad consequences for everyone.

It is possible that your children's personality and tastes might cause you to feel a certain empathy toward one or the other of them. It is normal that, depending on your own personality, you may get along better with one of your children's personality types.

However, as an adult, you must know how to relate well to all your children and support each one's personality, whatever it may be.

UNDERSTANDING DIFFERENT PERSONALITIES

Unlike physical traits, our children's personalities are not as quickly or easily apparent. Their personalities gradually come to light as we interact with them and observe how they react to different situations.

Have you ever watched or read Winnie-the-Pooh? Christopher Robin is a boy who plays with his stuffed animals, creating adventures in what he calls "The Hundred Acre Wood." Pooh, the bear, is the main character in these stories. He is always surrounded by friends, each with a distinct personality. Just like in real life, each of these characters interprets and resolves situations in their own unique way:

- **Pooh** is a sensitive, calm, and somewhat absentminded little bear. He is very curious and always open to new experiences.
- **Eeyore**, the donkey, always seems sad and has a rather negative outlook, though he is content with it. He is introverted and usually sees things differently from others.
- **Piglet**, the pig, enjoys life's simple pleasures—but not new things! He tends to get nervous about change. He is very sentimental and also worries about how others feel.
- **Rabbit** dislikes having his things disturbed. He is extremely organized and structured.
- **Tigger**, the tiger, is super energetic. He can't sit still or stay quiet, is very impulsive, and often gets into trouble. He is highly extroverted and always eager to show off his abilities.

Similarly, we find a wide variety of personalities within our own families. Just like Christopher Robin does, we must care for, respect, and love each person for who they are.

The more we understand our children's personalities, the better we can help them grow in a healthy way. We can also guide them in balancing the positive aspects of their personality with those that might create difficulties or limitations.

It's important that we observe our children closely so we can discover the special traits God has given each of them.

Many researchers have dedicated themselves to defining and categorizing different personality types. While it is well known that each person is unique, certain traits or qualities tend to be more predominant in some individuals than in others.

The 20th century brought significant advancements in this field, and English-American psychologist Raymond Cattell spent many years analyzing and measuring different personality traits based on how people respond to life's experiences.

One of his greatest contributions—widely accepted by professionals in the field—was the categorization of personality into five major measurable factors:

(Factor O): Openness to Experience

This factor answers the questions: How willing is the person to discover new experiences? How curious are they?

A person open to experience has a fluid relationship with their imagination, appreciates art and aesthetics, and is aware of their own emotions and those of the people around them. They prefer to break from routine and usually possess knowledge of a wide range of topics due to their great intellectual curiosity.

The opposite personality has more conventional interests. They enjoy simplicity more than complexity. They tend to see science or art as impractical disciplines. They prefer what is familiar over what is new and are attached to tradition.

A child who shows great openness to experience should be accompanied in their exploration of new things (while taking proper precautions). On the other hand, a child who is less inclined to this should be given confidence so they feel encouraged to explore their surroundings a bit more.

(Factor C): Conscientiousness

This factor answers the questions: How focused is the person on their goals? How disciplined are they in achieving them?

A person who scores high in this aspect is organized, has a high capacity for concentration, finishes their tasks, and thinks before making a decision.

If, on the other hand, we have a child with little discipline and who is very disorganized, we will need to help them with systems that remind them of the importance of order and find ways to motivate them to finish the tasks they start.

(Factor E): Extraversion

This factor answers the questions: How open is the person with others? How do they develop socially? Do they enjoy being surrounded by other people?

Those who score high in this factor are considered extroverted: they like to express themselves to others and enjoy socializing. They tend to be action-oriented.

The opposite is introversion, which is seen in people who are more reflective and less action-oriented than extroverts. These are very reserved individuals, so much so that they are often perceived as unfriendly. This type of person tends to be quite independent, often preferring to be alone, and choosing routine and the family environment over noisy, crowded places. But this does not mean they are less happy, and they can enjoy themselves greatly in small circles of friendship.

(Factor A): Agreeableness

This factor answers the question: How empathetic is the person toward the emotions and feelings of others?

Here the aim is to measure the degree to which a person is respectful, tolerant, and understanding toward the feelings of the one in front of them.

An agreeable person trusts in the honesty of others, and has a vocation to help and assist anyone in need, showing themselves to be humble and simple.

For example, children with a high score in this factor will notice their parents' moods even if they try to hide them. They may also be concerned if a sibling or a classmate is suffering and will look for ways to help them.

(Factor N): Emotional Stability

This factor answers the questions: How does the person react to crises or complicated situations? Do they get very upset, or do they tend to remain stable?

Calm people, not very prone to feeling anger or rage, usually stay cheerful at all times and manage their personal crises well.

For children who show low levels of emotional stability, we must teach them to better manage stress and frustration, and to use the right words instead of hitting or throwing things.

We must also keep in mind that the way children resolve their crises, in addition to being related to their personality, comes from learning based on what they observe. We are a fundamental point of reference for them. If children see their parents tending toward depression when facing difficulties, it is possible they will adopt this model. On the other hand, if children observe shouting, hitting, and fighting when adults resolve conflicts, they will likely believe this is the proper way to solve their own conflicts.

Returning to the topic of personality, I want to stress that there are no good or bad personalities. It is wrong to think that way. Personalities are the way each of us is designed to respond to social situations, to our responsibilities, to relationships with others, and to life's problems. Every personality has its strengths and weaknesses.

And as parents, we must help strengthen our children's strengths, but also help them with their weaknesses. The focus should also be on shaping their character: that they love what is right, that they speak the truth, that they fear the Lord, and that they pursue justice and mercy, regardless of the personality each one has. Our goal should not be to change them into our "ideal" version of a child, but to help each one be successful, developing within God's design the potential and unique characteristics He placed in them.

Chapter 04

ENEMIES OF IDENTITY

It is important to be aware that identity—which is based on what we know about ourselves through personal discovery and the information we receive from others—is vulnerable. When we have a distorted image of ourselves or of reality, it can lead to shyness, fear, or lack of action, among other things.

The way we as parents explain to our children who they are will largely depend on what we believe defines a person. In other words, what is it that makes you, as a mother, important and valuable?

As we reflect on this question, we may realize that we have been influenced by the values of today's society. Do we give more importance to having rather than being? Are we defined by status? By our profession, achievements, race, money, or beauty?

We are already grown. We have traveled a long road of learning, while our child is just beginning. Throughout our journey, we have learned to value and define ourselves—probably incorrectly. That is why we need to start with ourselves, clearing our minds of our own mistaken concepts.

My identity is what I am worth as a person, for my heart, for my essence.

My identity is what I am worth as a person, for my heart, for my essence.

When we strip away all the superficial things we use to define ourselves, we reach the core of what identity truly is. My identity is what I am worth as a person, for my heart, for my essence. No one can take my identity away from me.

That is why our focus on our children must always be on their being. Just as we have our own "enemies" of true identity, children have theirs too, and we must teach children about them so their true identity is protected and allowed to thrive.

1. Mistakes Parents Make

- **Rigidity and Fear**
  From the age of three onward, the world begins to open up to little ones. Their imagination soars, and they believe they can do and explore everything. If we, as mothers, are rigid or fearful, we will impose overly strict limits that prevent our children from exploring their capabilities. Perhaps our rigidity will even stop us from celebrating their achievements or offering them words of affirmation to help them push aside fear when they need to.

  Remember: Every opportunity we take to encourage our children to try something new opens doors to valuable lessons that will stay with them throughout their lives.

- **Perfectionism**
  Perfectionism, like rigidity, never celebrates anything. It is never satisfied with results and always feels that something is missing. A perfectionist mother is constantly sending the message to her child: "You're not good enough for..." Even if she doesn't say it explicitly, the child will clearly understand the message.

To make matters worse, if we are perfectionist mothers, we will also prevent our children from developing responsibility. By not assigning them tasks (because "It's better if I do it; you don't do it right"), they will end up doing nothing. But what if they are actually doing things well, just in a different way than we would?

Perfectionism hurts our children and can turn into an internal voice they will hear for the rest of their lives—a voice that tells them what they "should" be instead of recognizing and valuing who they actually are. In their minds, the thoughts that will constantly circulate might be:

"I should be like my brother."
"I should be good."
"I should be organized."
"I should understand better when something is explained to me."
"I should never have done this or that."

- **The Concept of the "Ideal Child"**

It is not good to try to guide (or force) them to be someone they are not.

Even before our children are born, we often have idealized images of what we want them to be. It is good and normal to have goals for our children. However, it is not good to try to guide (or force) them to be someone they are not. For example, making our child play a sport even if they don't like it, just because it is popular in our culture. Or forcing them to play an instrument because we dreamed of it when we were children and now want to compensate through our kids. Another example of pushing our children into something they are not is when we decide early on their profession: "Here comes the doctor who will take care of me when I'm old!" or "You're definitely going to be an engineer like your father and grandfather—it's a family tradition!"

When adults do this, children feel unconsciously bound to fulfill this "family mandate" and do what is expected of them, taking away their opportunity to explore what they actually want to be or do.

This doesn't only happen with professions. Some mothers might dream of having outgoing, confident children—kids who aren't afraid to speak in public or boldly take on new challenges. But what if our child is introverted and doesn't behave the way we expected? We might insist they "step up" or "be brave," making them believe that being introverted is a flaw and leading them to develop incorrect thought patterns about themselves.

The problem with the "ideal child" is that sooner or later they will clash with the real child we have. If we insist on an ideal, we miss out on discovering the potential our real child has.

The worst part is that when a child feels they don't live up to their parents' expectations, they may develop negative thought patterns that directly attack their identity: "I'm not good enough as I am," "Something must be wrong with me," or "I will never be able to do anything right."

2. Bullying

Bullying, or harassment, is the constant physical or psychological mistreatment a child receives from other children (who can also be family members) with the intent to dominate, intimidate, or obtain something from them, or simply to satisfy a need for aggression.

Bullying is a major problem in schools today. As parents, we must prepare our children to stand against it while also taking a firm stance against these attacks on our little ones.

It is also important to understand that if a child (whether our own or someone else's) grows up in a home with any form of violence, they may become the one initiating bullying against other children. These children subconsciously believe that there are only two types of people in relationships: the aggressor and the victim.

As mothers, we must become experts in detecting bullying early so we can address it right away. Bullying should never be ignored or tolerated. Depending on our child's personality, they may not tell us that it is happening. That's why it's crucial to ask them different questions about how they feel at school, how other children behave, and if there is anything that bothers or upsets them. Another way to detect bullying is to check for bruises or scratches. Observe their behavior when they respond—do they evade the question, get nervous, or look down?

But the issue doesn't stop there. Listening to our children is important, but taking action is even more crucial. Some cases can be resolved quickly by giving our children advice on how to defend themselves from bullying. However, if the problem persists despite their efforts, we need to take further steps:

- **If you detect bullying at home:** Apply firm discipline to stop the aggressor's behavior.
- **If you detect bullying at school:** Schedule a meeting with the teacher and report the case to the administration. Insist that protective measures be taken for your child and that appropriate action is taken toward the aggressor. If bullying does not stop, consider transferring your child to a different class—or even a different school if necessary.

Keep in mind that bullying is rarely the work of just one person. The bully will often recruit allies, making it harder for the victim to defend themselves because they face a "one against many" situation.

If your child is a victim of bullying, in addition to taking these steps, dedicate time to talk openly about it. Reinforce affirmations of self-worth and pray with them, reminding them that they are never alone because the Lord is always with them. Pray that no lies take root in their heart and that their physical integrity is always protected.

You can also share the following advice from Kids Health with your child:

- **Ignore the bullying.** Bullies seek a reaction, so not responding may stop the attacks.
- **Stand firm.** You may not feel braver or stronger than them, but when treated badly, speak up firmly: "Enough!" or "NO MORE!" Then, report the incident to an authority figure as quickly as possible. Even if you don't feel confident, act with confidence to stop manipulation or aggression.
- **Find friends who support you.** Remember, two are better than one. Avoid being alone with those who intend to harm you, especially if the bullying is physical.
- **Do not fight back.** Responding with aggression is not the answer—just as others should not harm you, you should not harm them.
- **Tell an adult.** This is the right thing to do, even if the bully calls you names for it. Reporting bullying is not about weakness but about preventing further harm.

3. The Spiritual Enemy

In his second letter to the Corinthians, the apostle Paul warns that the enemy has schemes, plans, and intentions against us, which we must not ignore (2 Corinthians 2:11). We must be alert so we can defend ourselves and not fall into his traps. In Paul's case, he asks the church to forgive, comfort, and welcome back a person who had done wrong and seemed to have repented "so that he will not be overwhelmed by excessive sorrow" (v. 7).

The Bible tells us that above all else, we must guard our hearts, because everything we do flows from it (Proverbs 4:23). The enemy knows this too. Both good and evil originate from the heart. It just depends on what we allow in.

One of the enemy's tactics is to attack us from an early age by planting false thoughts that eventually take root in our hearts. That's why it's so important for us, as mothers, to be attentive and protect our children from these deceptions. How do we do this? By listening carefully to what they say. Instead of scolding them quickly when they express something incorrectly, we should take the time to understand their thoughts. Through their words we may uncover the enemy's trap meant to damage their hearts. By listening carefully, we can lovingly help correct their mistaken beliefs.

For example, a child might say: "Why am I always punished unfairly?" Our first instinct might be to respond harshly: "What do you mean I'm unfair?" But we should pause. The point is not whether they are right but that they feel an injustice. Instead of reprimanding them immediately, this is a moment to ask more questions.

Similarly, if we hear them murmur things like: "I'll never be good enough", "I'm not smart enough", "I'm not a good son/daughter", "I always misbehave", or "I'm just a bad kid." This is the time to sit with them, talk, and teach them God's truth about their worth. By doing this, we ensure that these lies are uprooted before they take deep root in their hearts.

HOW DOES THE ENEMY ATTACK OUR CHILDREN?

The enemy's strategies against our children are the same as those he uses against us, primarily:

- **Instilling fear**
  Fear is a weapon used to shake our faith. Someone once described fear as faith placed in the wrong thing. The enemy wants us to take our eyes off God, weakening our trust in Him so that we become paralyzed and intimidated.

Throughout history, empires used fear as a means of control. When conquering new lands, they would display acts of cruelty to subdue people through intimidation.

Proclaiming what the spirit reminds us of is a cure for fear.

Fear paralyzes us, preventing us from walking in the truth of who we really are. That's why, Mama, we must be very mindful of fear's impact. How We Speak to Our Children Matters. Be mindful of the way you speak to your children. Don't instill fear by telling them scary stories, like "If you don't sleep now, the boogeyman will come for you." Don't threaten them with consequences like "The police will take you away if you misbehave." Also, be cautious of what they hear from others, what they watch on TV, and the conversations around them. Do not give the enemy an opportunity to plant fear in your children. Instead, listen attentively to their fears and immediately restore their confidence in the Lord. Find Bible verses that they can learn from an early age, and train them in how to fight and defend themselves.

Remember, against fear we have been given two weapons of war: the shield and the sword. The shield, as Paul says in Ephesians 6:16, is faith–which represents everything you know about God. This is the truth that must be carried into every battle when facing fear.

What do your children know about God? Do they know that He is almighty, invincible, that He never leaves us alone, that He loves us, and that nothing evil can touch us because, like a good shepherd, He protects us even in the face of death threats? If they do not know these truths, you must teach them! Fear vanishes in the presence of the Lord's proclaimed truth. That is why praise is so powerful–it declares who God is!

The second weapon we have is the sword. Paul tells us in Ephesians 6:17 that this is the sword of the Spirit, which is the Word of God. Read the Bible with your children every day. Memorize Bible verses together. Fill their hearts and minds with God's Word. This will be extremely useful on the day of battle, because proclaiming what the Spirit reminds us from Scripture destroys fear.

One night, my daughter, Victoria, couldn't sleep and called me, visibly distressed. She said, "Please pray for me. Every time I close my eyes, I see scary things, and I get afraid." Instead of simply praying for her, I saw it as an opportunity to teach her. I told her that while I always prayed for her, this time, I would teach her to defend herself. I reminded her that she had memorized Psalm 23, and now she needed to personalize it and make it her own. I explained, "When you say this Psalm, see yourself as the little sheep." Then, I guided her through it: "The Lord is my shepherd; I lack nothing He makes me lie down in green pastures" *(imagine running through those green fields)*. "He leads me beside quiet waters" *(imagine drinking from those peaceful waters).* "He refreshes my soul; I have no fear because you take care of me, Lord." When we reached the verse "Even though I walk through the darkest valley..." I told Victoria, "Now, raise your voice and declare: 'I will fear no evil, for You are with me!'" When we finished, she had a big smile on her face and said, "Thank you, Mom! That was such a victory!"

I wish I could tell you that Victoria never felt fear again, but the truth is that she had similar experiences later. However, this was a good thing because it gave me another chance to remind her how to respond to fear and reinforce in her the truth that the Lord has already given us victory.

- **Replacing Lies with Truth**

It is just as important to teach our children to think correctly as it is to teach them responsibility for their actions.

In John 10:10, Jesus warned us that Satan acts according to his nature: He is a liar, a murderer, and a thief. His goal is to kill our faith and steal what belongs to us. His main strategy is to make us believe lies about who we are and who God is.

2 Corinthians 10:3-5 teaches that our mind is the battlefield where spiritual warfare happens. Paul explains that strongholds are built there—false arguments and rebellious thoughts that rise against the knowledge of God and His truth. That's why Paul urges us to take every thought captive and make it obedient to Christ.

Even though the enemy is not responsible for all our bad actions, he does play a role by planting the seeds of lies in us. We, however, are responsible for what we allow to grow in our minds. We must take responsibility and decide what we will allow to take root. Teaching our children to take responsibility for their thoughts is crucial. They must be encouraged to think correctly, because the Bible says that a person is a product of their thoughts (Proverbs 23:7). If they have negative thoughts about themselves, they will act accordingly. But if they believe they are precious and deeply loved children of God, they will grow up confident and secure in their identity.

DO NOT JOIN THE ENEMY'S VOICE!

The difference between the enemy's voice and the Holy Spirit's voice is clear: The enemy condemns. "You're a failure.", "You're worthless." But the Holy Spirit speaks truth in love: "What you did was wrong, but here's how you can make it right.", "Apologize to

We must strive for our voice to resemble the holy spirit's, always speaking to our children with encouragement, love, and hope.

your friend.", "Draw closer to God to overcome this struggle." The Holy Spirit's voice gives hope and a way forward.

How Do You Speak to Your Child? When your child misbehaves, do your words bring condemnation, or do they offer love and hope? Children make mistakes, just like we do, but they are not defined by their mistakes. Their mistakes aren't their identity. We need to help recognize the difference between their core character in God, which is always the same, and their sometimes behavior, which they can learn from and change. They are not messy–sometimes they make messes. They are not liars–sometimes they don't tell the truth. They are not rude–sometimes they behave rudely. That is the enemy's voice, trying to label them and harm their identity. Our voices, as mothers, must never sound like the enemy's! We must always speak words of encouragement, love, and hope–helping our children find a way out instead of making them feel trapped in their behavior.

When I correct my daughter, I am careful with my words because I know the Holy Spirit has warned me about the importance of speaking appropriately. If I see a mess in her room, I say: "It's pretty messy here; you need to clean up." If she misbehaves, I tell her: "That is the wrong attitude, and I won't let it slide." Or, "You're choosing to lie, and that is not right. Choose the truth instead."

Children often associate discipline with their worth or how much they are loved. As parents, we must show our children that our love is never in doubt. Children Must Know They Are Loved No Matter What. Our children must know that we don't love them more when they behave well and don't love them less when they misbehave. We love them simply because they are our children–and that will never change.

However, we must also explain that we love them so much that we won't allow them to continue making mistakes. If my daughter says, "I'm a bad girl," I correct her: "No, you are an amazing girl, but we need to fix that attitude." Another phrase I use: "You have such a beautiful heart, and I won't let you ruin it with that selfish attitude."

Moms, the Holy Spirit helps you when you feel weak. Teach your children that this same truth applies to them! When they say, "I try to be good, but I can't!", believe them—because you know the struggle yourself. Then, teach them to ask the Holy Spirit for help. Encourage them to walk with God and depend on Him always. This is the only way to keep them away from harm—both for them and for you.

Chapter 05

WHAT REALLY MATTERS

"Being confident of this, that he who began a good work in you will carry it on to completion until the day of Christ Jesus."
Philippians 1:6 (NIV)

All good mothers have the goal of securing a better future for their children. The question is, do we truly know what they need for that better future? We work excessively, sacrificing time with them to give them better things—like a bigger house, toys we never had, the best education, and more. However, in striving to provide what we believe they need most, we risk losing them in the process! Our children long for and need our presence, our attention, our affirmation, and our guidance—things that money can never replace.

In 2017, we experienced a major flood caused by Hurricane Harvey, which struck Houston with several days of intense rain. Because of the damage, we couldn't immediately return to our home, and while we repaired it we had to rent a small apartment. We furnished it with only the essentials and, of course, with Victoria's favorite toys—the ones we managed to save. Our main focus was ensuring stability for our daughter. We hung up her pictures and decorated her new room with familiar things, trying to make her transition to the temporary home as smooth as possible.

Adults work so hard to afford big houses so their children can be "more comfortable," when in reality, what they truly desire is to be close to us.

Not even a week had passed when she said, "Mom, Dad, I like this apartment so much more than our house!" We were surprised by her comment. When we asked why, she said, "It's because now my playroom is in the living room, so we're all together!" She preferred the small apartment over the big house because it kept us all in the same space. She was right there with me while I prepared dinner and Dad studied. There were no walls separating her playroom from the kitchen or Dad's office. We were all together, each doing our own tasks. Adults work so hard to afford big houses so their children can be "more comfortable," when in reality, what they truly desire is to be close to us.

What a great lesson Hurricane Harvey taught us! We adults strive to buy big houses so our children have space and there's no mess of toys in the living room. But in reality, what they want most is to be near us, to have us play with them or at least watch them play. They long for us!

When we finally returned to our house, we decided to simplify the spaces and arrange them differently, making sure to always stay close to one another. Little Victoria had helped us see what truly mattered.

Maybe you don't have the "good problem" of living in Texas, where most houses are very large. Maybe you're constantly trying to manage the problem of limited space and keeping things organized. I just want to tell you to be careful about what you wish for and what you chase after. Perhaps right now you have a great opportunity to be near your children, but you're not valuing it. Even if they scream, argue, and make a mess, remember that it's only for a short time—a time that will pass quickly. And as it does, they long for you to be there to celebrate their victories, help them solve their problems, encourage them when they face challenges, and show them your love and interest in what they do, building strong and healthy bonds.

SOME BASIC PRINCIPLES FOR SHAPING OUR CHILDREN'S CHARACTER

Character is one of the main qualities that define a person's identity. Here, I refer to character as the set of principles, values, and virtues that each human being holds. Unlike personality, character is learned and shaped. While some virtues may be innate, most must be intentionally adopted.

Character is like the rails on which a person's life runs—it affects their way of thinking, acting, and reacting, their desires, and their relationships with others. In other words, character influences all areas of life.

We've just mentioned virtues and values, and it's important to distinguish between the two:

- Values are things that a person recognizes, accepts, and lives by as good for their life. A value is whatever one deems important, desirable, or necessary. For example, some people place great value on owning a beautiful car, while others do not. For some people truth has a very high value, while for others, not so much.

A value can be identified by answering the question: What do you love or pursue most intensely in life? Money, wisdom, or doing what pleases God are some possible answers. Although we all have values, each home establishes its scale of priorities. In other words, while everyone may value the same thing, the level of importance each assigns to it varies.

- Virtue is the strength that enables good actions. Virtues come from God, as stated in James 1:17: "Every good and perfect gift is from above, coming down from the Father of the heavenly lights."

Some virtues are innate—we are born with traces of God's nature, like patience and kindness. Others, however, must be developed by practicing them, being intentional, and prioritizing them.

When it comes to morality, due to the sinful nature we struggle with, we face the dilemma Paul describes in Romans 7:18: "For I have the desire to do what is good, but I cannot carry it out." This is where the power of the Holy Spirit intervenes. As we walk with Him and desire to do good but struggle to do so, the Spirit makes virtues "come alive" in us as fruits and evidence of His presence in our lives. Love, joy, peace, patience, kindness, goodness, faithfulness, humility, and self-control are all virtues or fruits that the Holy Spirit produces in us (Galatians 5:22-23).

THE RESPONSIBILITY OF TEACHING OUR CHILDREN ABOUT MORALITY IS OURS

With the many commitments we parents have today, the task of intentionally teaching our children about morality becomes increasingly difficult. What do we do then? Do we delegate this responsibility to others?

Raising our children to be men and women of God should come from daily living, not just a weekly visit to church.

Today, society is one of the greatest influencers of children and youth. We have given it this power. Our children adopt the values and principles they see on TV and YouTube. While they are young, certain values like respect, tolerance, and teamwork are highlighted in children's programming. But as they grow older, we see how popularity, beauty, skill, and the "me first" mentality become their top priorities.

Another place where we tend to delegate this responsibility is in educational institutions. However, we must remember that each institution follows its own set of values. While excellence, respect, and responsibility are often emphasized, their primary mission is to prepare individuals for professional and social life, rather than nurturing their hearts and other essential aspects of their lives. Raising our children to be men and women of God should come from daily living, not just a weekly visit to church. The other place where we tend to delegate our kids' formation is the church. We believe (and I wish it were true!) that taking our children faithfully to Sunday school will make them men and women of God. Of course, the church will expose them to these teachings, but ultimately, the responsibility of shaping their character and values falls on us as parents.

YOU CANNOT TEACH WHAT YOU ARE NOT

The commitment to raising our children to be men and women of good moral character requires us to truly live out the values we want them to learn.

The commitment to raising our children to be men and women of good moral character requires us to truly live out the values we want them to learn.

When it comes to teaching morality, the challenge becomes even greater because it requires us to be what we teach our children is morally right. When they see us find a lost phone and say, "Lucky me!" instead of trying to return it, we are teaching them about morality. When they hear us bribing a police officer who pulled us over for speeding, we are teaching them about morality. When they hear us lying on the phone, we are teaching them about morality. If we want to raise them as children of God who love the things of God, we ourselves must love God and be consistent in our actions. This means honoring Him in our home, attending and serving in church, honoring Him with our finances, and reflecting His values in all our relationships. It may be a great effort, but I assure you, it will be worth it!

By instilling in our children the virtues and values of God's kingdom, we give them a foundation that will shape their lives.

Below is a list of virtues, along with practical advice on how to teach each one to our children.

LOVE

This is the virtue of virtues and the value of values. It is not just a feeling–it is an action! The Golden Rule should be our guiding principle in all relationships: We must always treat others as we would like to be treated.

Love also has its order:

- First, to God
- Second, to myself
- Third, to others

These are the principles we must consistently reinforce in our children as they grow, taking every opportunity to instill them. Instead of simply saying, "Forgive your friend," we should go further and take the time to explain, "Do you know why we should forgive? Because it pleases God and because we also like to be forgiven when we make mistakes."

Love is also the driving force behind all other values. The apostle Paul makes it clear in 1 Corinthians 13 that all virtues are meaningless if we lack love.

TRUTH

A key to knowing what values to instill at home is to ask: What values does God have? In other words, what does God love? Let's take a look:

- God loves truth in the inner being. (Psalm 51:6)
- He loves justice, and those who love justice will see His face. (Psalm 11:7)
- The Lord loves His children, and that is why He corrects them. (Hebrews 12:6)

Truth is also proof that we are children of God, not of Satan, who is the father of lies. We must encourage our children to be honest despite the consequences and instill in them the belief that truth is for strong and special people–those who are brave!

We must be cautious of the temptation to lie to "help" our children out of trouble. Statements like "I'll get you a doctor's note to excuse your absence" should never be heard in a Christian home.

Speaking of courage, let's revisit the idea from the previous chapter about the armor of God that helps us stand against the enemy (Ephesians 6:14). Remember, and remind your children, that the belt of this armor is "the belt of truth." Truth is what holds the armor of God together and allows it to continuously offer protection over our lives!

JOY

This is the virtue that keeps you cheerful and hopeful regardless of the circumstances. It is the strength that comes from finding the source of happiness in God.

It is a concept difficult to achieve even for adults, but you can teach your child that one of the things he must guard most is to

It is the strength that comes from finding the source of happiness in God.

not let anything take away his joy. That is why teaching him to manage his anger and frustration is very important.

When my daughter gets upset with someone or something, we like to remind her that when she holds on to the feeling of anger (which is a normal and necessary reaction, but shouldn't last too long), it is stealing her joy. This way, we are teaching her that she is the only owner of her heart, and that she can choose the best option.

Sadness is also a thief of joy. When a child is sad, it is an alert that something is not right, and as parents we must find out the cause. Perhaps you, as a mother, may have some idea of what is causing your child sadness, but it is still better to ask and insist until he himself can talk about what is happening to him.

Tiredness in children (as well as in adults) is also a source of irritability and also robs us of joy. Sometimes, with the family schedules being so busy, we do not give our children enough time to rest. Let's be careful not to overload them with too many extra-curricular activities. Children should have free time to play, and also to rest the necessary hours.

How can we cultivate joy in our children? When we teach them to fix their eyes on God and on the things He can do in the midst of difficult situations, we are showing them optimism and hope, and that helps to cultivate joy and gladness in their lives. If your family or your child is going through difficult situations, it would be good to go over the story of Moses and the Hebrew people when they came out of Egypt. When they found themselves trapped by the Egyptian army that was pursuing them, God opened a way where no one imagined: through the sea. When they had no food, God sent manna from heaven for their daily sustenance. Telling our children these stories, and believing that He will help us too, can bring joy and gladness to the soul even in difficult times.

Depression is something that in recent times has been affecting many young people, and even children. When they cannot find resources in their soul to sustain themselves, when they do not know how to fight against the sadness produced by adverse situations, they feel that everything turns dark and the horizon closes in and hope runs out. What a different outlook it would be if they could turn to God and enjoy the joy that only He can give!

PEACE

The role of mothers is key to keeping the home in peace.

The role of mothers is key to keeping the home in peace.

This is the strength that keeps us calm even in situations of conflict.

The role of mothers is key to keeping the home in peace.

Let's take care of the atmosphere in our home! Let's not raise our voices so quickly. Let's not get upset over things that are not that important. Let's also not allow fear to take hold of us and rob us of peace.

This is exactly what the apostle Peter invites us to when he says:

"Rather, it should be that of your inner self, the unfading beauty of a gentle and quiet spirit, which is of great worth in God's sight." (1 Peter 3:4, NIV)

One of the things that robs us of peace is stress, which is the anxiety over everything we have to face. The problem is that stress never stays inside us. It always finds a way out, putting others on edge as well.

If this is your case, nowadays there is a lot of advice on how to eliminate stress, from making quick adjustments to your life to exercising more. However, the advice the Scriptures give us is both effective and simple: first come before the Lord, put everything in prayer, and give thanks for all He has done. When we remember what God has done in the past, both in our own life and in the stories we read in His Word, this restores our peace and affirms us in the confidence that the Lord takes care of our life and our family!

Paul puts it this way:

"Do not be anxious about anything, but in every situation, by prayer and petition, with thanksgiving, present your requests to God. And the peace of God, which transcends all understanding, will guard your hearts and your minds in Christ Jesus." (Philippians 4:6-7, NIV)

As a mom, you should be attentive to identify what things are robbing your children of peace or instilling fear in them, so you can help them. Here I share some tips that may be useful:

Do not make the mistake of arguing with your spouse in front of the children. This is a very common cause of fear, and it creates in children a sense of instability.

Control what they watch on television, especially in the month of October, when most children's programming is about monsters, ghosts, witches, etc.

Do not allow siblings to tell each other scary stories, especially because the youngest ones cannot distinguish between reality and fantasy. Opening the door to fear in our children's lives is giving the enemy a weapon to attack them.

Help your children memorize Bible verses that keep them in peace. For example, if they have trouble sleeping at night, memorize together: "In peace I will lie down and sleep, for you alone, Lord, make me dwell in safety." (Psalm 4:8, NIV)

Conflictive relationships also rob us of peace. Seek quick reconciliation, and choose carefully which battles are worth fighting. There is a saying: "Better a bad agreement than a good fight." This is what Abraham did with his nephew Lot when the herders of each of them quarreled over the pasture for the sheep. Abraham decided that Lot would choose first, and of course, Lot chose the best pasture. But Abraham knew that his blessing was not going to come from grabbing the best land, but from trusting in God. And that's how it was! God always prospered Abraham, while Lot, after becoming wealthy, lost everything he had.

To help them avoid conflicts, you can memorize this verse with your children: "It is to one's honor to avoid strife, but every fool is quick to quarrel." (Proverbs 20:3, NIV)

Finally, there are other types of things that can rob us of peace. Here I mean situations of illness, threats, or calamities. In the face of these, Jesus promised us:

"I have told you these things, so that in me you may have peace. In this world you will have trouble. But take heart! I have overcome the world." (John 16:33, NIV)

Jesus also said that when we work for peace we are called children of God. Memorize this verse together: "Blessed are the peacemakers, for they will be called children of God." (Matthew 5:9, NIV)

Finally, let us strive, as mothers, to be people who seek peace, both with our words and with our daily actions. Our example is the best teaching we can give our children.

PATIENCE

This is the virtue that helps us endure and wait on God. As our little ones mature, our goal should be to teach them that things don't always have to happen right now.

We must have patience:

- **With ourselves:** This has to do with giving ourselves the time to achieve what we desire, with persevering, with trying again and again, and with being tolerant in the face of frustration.

- **With others:** This has to do with "gracefully enduring" people in their weaknesses. We teach our children this virtue when we do not allow siblings to mock one another or use rude labels that demean the other.

  Share these verses with your children:
  "Whoever is patient has great understanding, but one who is quick-tempered displays folly." (Proverbs 14:29, NIV)

  "Better a patient person than a warrior, one with self-control than one who takes a city." (Proverbs 16:32, NIV)

  With our desires: The main reason people go into debt is that they cannot wait to save up for the things they want. ("Why wait if I can have it now?") Not being patient can get us into a lot of trouble and add unnecessary stress to our lives. We foster patience in our children when wc teach them the value of saving, and when we show them they can achieve their goals with determination and one step at a time—just like a farmer does with his crops.

  Share these verses with your children:

  "Be still before the Lord and wait patiently for him; do not fret when people succeed in their ways, when they carry out their wicked schemes." (Psalm 37:7, NIV)

  "Be patient, then, brothers and sisters, until the Lord's coming. See how the farmer waits for the land to yield its valuable crop, patiently waiting for the autumn and spring rains." (James 5:7, NIV)

1. Establish the value of money in your family

As we said above, the proper or improper handling of money is closely related to patience. In addition, it takes children some time to understand the value of money and how transactions work.

When she was younger, my daughter saw the card I used for shopping as if it were a "magic wand" that made things pass from the store to our home. I realized this when I once told her: "We don't have money for that," and she replied: "But you still have the card in your wallet!" Explaining to her how the financial and commercial circuit works, and what the purpose of money is, was not an easy task. That's why I set out to find the best way to do it, and here I share some things I learned in the process...

In Matthew 25:14-30, Jesus tells a parable about a man who entrusted different amounts of talents (the currency of the time) to three of his servants. To one he gave 5, and this one put them to work and returned 10. To another he gave 2, and this one also doubled the amount, returning 4. But to the last one he gave 1, and this one, instead of putting it to work, buried it and, after a time, returned the same talent to the master. Jesus says that the master rebuked the one who produced nothing with his money, took it away from him, and gave it to the one who had the most.

To be honest, I must confess that I always thought with a mistaken sense of justice and would ask myself why the master had not given that talent to the one who had 2. However, now I see that the teaching is clear: the more faithful we are in the administration and correct use of resources, the more prepared we will be to handle greater amounts. Otherwise, having money can become a calamity.

Dave Ramsey is an authority in the United States on the topic of money. He has some very good material that I bought to use with Victoria. It is very simple and helps us teach children some basic principles:

- **Money is earned with effort**
  Ramsey suggests that according to their age, and even from a very young age, you assign your children chores or responsibilities at home, and reward them at the end of the week with a set amount. Each task should have an amount assigned to it. He suggests making a chart with each child's name, their tasks, a space to mark if they completed them or not, and at the end of the week, how much they earned.

In Latin America, it is customary to give children an "allowance," which is a set amount of money for them to use on treats or snacks. Now that I live in the United States, many times I have asked successful business parents how they teach their children to handle money. I was surprised when one told me: "I don't give my children an allowance because that would create in them the mentality of living off government aid. I assign them a task, and I pay them for it. This way I highlight the value of work and its reward."

It's no wonder I see teenagers here in the U.S. mowing lawns, working in stores or restaurants from the age of 16, delivering newspapers, or babysitting while their parents go out. Quite an interesting contrast, right?
Of course, it's worth clarifying that not all household chores should be paid. Certain chores should be assigned to each child to create a sense of responsibility and care for the home, which belongs to everyone. As part of being a family, we all work together.

But there are other chores that can be paid. Here is a small chart with some good ideas:

(It goes without saying that we must be very careful when assigning tasks that could put the child's safety at risk. No sharp knives, being near fire, or going out in the street without supervision while still young.)

Children 3–4 years	**Children 6–7 years**	**Children 8–10 years**
Make the bed	Sort laundry	Any of the previous tasks, plus:
Dust	Put away clean clothes	Load the dishwasher

Feed the pets	Take out the trash	Vacuum
Empty wastebaskets	Help pack snacks	Help wash the car
Set or clear the table	Keep room tidy	Put away groceries

2. The three purposes of money

Ramsey also teaches that it's a good idea for each child to have three jars labeled as follows:

- **Give:** From an early age we must explain to our children that we are not owners of anything but merely stewards of what God gives us, and that one of the purposes of our money is to show generosity to those most in need. We must teach them to set aside a part of what they have to give to others, as well as 10% to give as tithes. We must teach them that we are generous with others because our Heavenly Father is generous, and that we honor Him with our tithes because God's house is our spiritual home, and we are responsible for caring for and maintaining it.
- **Save**: Savings can have as their goal something special that our child desires. This way, we are teaching patience, and to enjoy the fruit of having worked and waited for what they longed for.
- **Spend:** This is the jar from which the child will take money for sweets, or later to go to the movies or to a park with friends. (By the way, this is a good point to teach our child to distinguish between wants and needs, which are not the same. A valuable lesson that will serve them for life!)

KINDNESS

This is the strength that makes you treat others well. It includes good manners, respect, and the courteous way of asking for things. It means being someone who knows how to honor other people: authorities, elders, siblings, those who work in our homes, etc. Kindness dignifies people simply because they are fellow human beings before God.

Establish in your family the value of respect

Do not allow your children to use rude manners, tones that sound demanding, to hurt others with words, or to use bad or crude language. All of this goes against being kind, and you must help your children avoid these behaviors.

Establish in your family the value of tolerance

It is important to understand that there are different definitions of tolerance, and many of them are incorrect. This is something we need to be clear about in order to teach it correctly to our children. Tolerance is the recognition that we all have differences (both moral and religious). But it is not agreeing with or accepting someone else's dogma or opinion. This is where the definition becomes confusing, because some claim that people should live in harmony by "softening their convictions."

A good definition is this: "Tolerance allows for healthy coexistence between people of different opinions under the agreement of respect and friendship."

As Christian mothers, we must raise a generation with firm and clear convictions, not children who accept any doctrine as good just because someone else says it is good. What we should teach them is not to attack or look down on someone because they think differently.

FAITHFULNESS

This is the strength or virtue of fulfilling promises.

Many times we make promises because, in the moment we make them, we feel or see great possibilities of achieving them. However, when situations change and the conditions are no longer as favorable as when we made the promise, only if we are faithful will we remain in fulfilling it.

Faithfulness goes hand in hand with another virtue called "diligence," because in its highest sense, diligence is the care and attention given to carrying out something.

Faithfulness includes three aspects:

- **We are faithful or diligent with God** when we fulfill the commitment we have made with His Word and His commandments.

  "God is not unjust; he will not forget your work and the love you have shown him as you have helped his people and continue to help them." (Hebrews 6:10, NIV)

  As mothers, we model faithfulness to God to our children...

  × when from a young age they see that we honor God with our money.

  × when we settle in a church and serve in it.

  × when we live what we preach, and in our daily actions they see that we are committed to God's Word.

- **We are faithful or diligent with ourselves** when we overcome laziness with this virtue.

  "Whoever can be trusted with very little can also be trusted with much, and whoever is dishonest with very little will also be dishonest with much." (Luke 16:10, NIV)

As mothers, we model faithfulness to ourselves to our children...

× when they see us set goals and meet them on time.

× when we work hard and respond to our work obligations with care, pursuing excellence.

- **We are faithful or diligent with others** when we take care with the actions we do with and toward them, and when we are trustworthy people who do not deceive or betray others.

"The Lord detests lying lips, but he delights in people who are trustworthy." (Proverbs 12:22, NIV)

As mothers, we model faithfulness to others to our children...

× when we are not hypocritical, speaking badly about others and then pretending otherwise when we are with them.

× when we do not cheat in games.

× when we keep the promises we make to them. (If at some point circumstances prevent us from keeping them, we must apologize and assure them we will fulfill them another time.)

Establish in your family the value of faithfulness

In ancient times, important agreements were made under oath before witnesses. Even the phrase "I give you my word" carried more weight than a signature does today because it was a matter of honor. Sadly, today, a person's word seems to be the least credible, and important agreements are mostly signed before a notary or a judge, in the presence of witnesses, with clauses setting out the consequences in case we do not keep what was promised.

Faithfulness is related to fulfilling promises, duty, and responsibility. Even within families, it is the glue that holds people together in times of crisis. However, nowadays it is sadly common to see how easily and quickly the promises made on a wedding day are forgotten. With parents abandoning their families or the increasingly common cases of infidelity, children can grow up with a very poor understanding of this virtue, even repeating family patterns unless the value of faithfulness is intentionally instilled as a pillar in their hearts and lives.

HUMILITY

This is the strength or virtue that recognizes our own limitations and weaknesses and acts according to that knowledge. It has been called the mother of virtues because only humility allows us to see who we really are, who God is, and what He can do in us.

Humility is one of the most difficult virtues to embrace because, unlike the others, it apparently does not make us "look" very good. It directly confronts the ego we all have. However, it is a virtue that greatly benefits us because "it allows us to learn from the past, act with confidence in the present, and have hope for the future."

In this sense, humility always positively affects those who are by your side or under your care.

The opposite of humility is pride and arrogance, and this is a problem because it attracts destruction. "Pride goes before destruction, a haughty spirit before a fall." (Proverbs 16:18, NIV)

It is true that low self-esteem is a problem we don't want our children to suffer. But, on the other extreme, it is also a problem for them to have a false or overly high self-esteem, based on something they are not.

The theologian and ancient history scholar John Dickson defines humility as the virtue of common sense, because no one is an expert in everything. We must admit the areas where we can be taught, and also learn to value and highlight the strengths of

Humility is the attitude Christ asks us to imitate so we can be guided by Him.

others to work well together as a team.

Humility is the attitude Christ asks us to imitate so we can be guided by Him.

Humility is the attitude Christ asks us to imitate in order to be guided by Him. One time my husband explained it in a teaching on humility, comparing it to a tamed horse: although it has the strength to go wherever it wants, it yields its will and offers its strength to someone else to be guided.

If your child embraces this attitude, you will guarantee their success in life. They will be someone who knows how to accept corrections and take the necessary steps to walk in the right direction.

Peter was the most impulsive of all the apostles of Jesus. Yet in the later years of his life, he wrote the following counsel about interpersonal relationships:

"...All of you, clothe yourselves with humility toward one another, because, 'God opposes the proud but shows favor to the humble.'" (1 Peter 5:5, NIV)

Now think for a moment about your child: Is he or she quick to apologize when disciplined for a fault? Do they accept advice and correction? What do they say about themselves? Do they constantly say they are better than others?

If you notice your child is having difficulties in the area of humility, help them as soon as possible! There are many good stories and resources available that talk about humility and can help strengthen it in your child.

SELF-CONTROL

This is the ability that allows us to control ourselves and our emotions, instead of letting them control us and rob us of the possibility of choosing what we want to feel at every moment of our lives. Prudence and temperance are synonyms of self-control.

Self-control is a manifestation of a good, firm character, and it indicates much maturity. That our children begin to practice this virtue from a young age will be a great advantage and a treasure for the rest of their lives–mainly because it will keep them out of a lot of trouble!

We can begin teaching them from childhood, when we don't give in to their tantrums or fits. The recommended approach is not to give them what they ask for when they ask for it rudely or with a bad attitude. On the contrary, reward and celebrate them when they show control over their emotions and their way of speaking.

Possessing this virtue truly is a strength of character that applies to all areas of our lives: we must have self-control with our money (this also applies to what we saw a few pages ago on money management), self-control in our relationships, and self-control with our tongue. As a mom, you must be intentional in teaching your children to have self-control in each of these areas!

For example, to teach them about the importance of controlling their tongue, read James 3 with them. There you will find many metaphors that children can understand. We are told that the tongue is like a ship's rudder, like a spark of fire, and many other interesting things. The apostle also points out the irony that man can tame all kinds of animals but not his tongue. When we can control what we say, it is a great achievement!

As we said before, prudence is related to self-control. A prudent person has the ability to think before speaking. They analyze whether a comment is beneficial, or if it is better to remain silent. A prudent person is also careful with their decisions and thinks carefully about their future:

"The prudent see danger and take refuge, but the simple keep going and pay the penalty." (Proverbs 27:12, NIV)

We have now reached the end of our list. All these virtues and values will lead us to define the most important thing about a person: their character, what it truly is.

John Maxwell explains in one of his books on leadership the difference between reputation and character. He says that reputation is what is known about a person, while character is the integrity that truly comes to light over time. Reputation is what someone has the moment they get a job, while character is what that person demonstrates after a year of being there. Clearly, character is more important, because: "If I take care of my character, my reputation will take care of itself."

Although people may try to appear to have good character in their work or social circles, sooner or later their true character will come to light. Sadly, it is often in the family environment where people are known for who they really are, due to closeness and the amount of time spent together. Let's strive to raise healthy children who are not double-minded. Children who grow into adults known for their virtues, both inside and outside their homes.

Chapter 06

PARENTING AND DISCIPLINE

The goal of every good parent is for their children to reach adulthood as mature individuals capable of making good decisions. The task of raising them correctly is one of the most delicate and complex. Parents often repeat the parenting or correction methods they experienced in their childhood because. Even if they promised not to treat their children the same way, when faced with the challenges of parenthood, they resort to what they know. On the other hand, some parents do the opposite of what their parents did because of the traumas they experienced.

Discipline is a nuanced topic, and none of our households will look exactly like anyone else's. It will depend on the personalities of the parents and the children. It will depend on how mom and dad were raised. It will also depend on cultural beliefs and how involved they believe the father should be in matters concerning the children (whether he will participate in decisions or only step in to "execute" a punishment when the mother cannot).

For many centuries, parenting and discipline responsibilities have fallen on the mother, as she was the parent spending the most time with the children. Today, although a large number of women work outside the home and childcare is often left to third parties, women still have the most daily contact with the children. Still, the responsibility of raising and correcting children has always been and will always be shared by both parents.

DIFFERENT TYPES OF PARENTS

The study of interpersonal relationships has established different types of parents based on several key factors, including their ability to show affection, their stance on discipline and order, their level of control, and the type of communication they establish. Based on the intensity of these factors, parents can generally be classified into the following types:

- **Authoritarian or Dominant Parents**

  These parents have a high degree of control and strictness but show little affection and have poor communication with their children.

  They tend to produce the most negative qualities in children. A harsh relationship will provoke resistance, secrecy, or rebellion in the children.

- **Permissive Parents**

  These parents are affectionate and communicate well with their children but are not very demanding and have little control over them. They are weak in setting and enforcing rules.

  One of the reasons they are so permissive is their fear of harming their children if they are too strict. These parents will provide a lot of emotional support to their children but will raise them without discipline, leading to children who are rude and capricious.

There is a verse in the book of Proverbs that addresses those who do not wish to correct:

"He who spares the rod hates his son, but he who loves him disciplines him early." (Proverbs 13:24)

- **Neglectful or Indifferent Parents**

They have low levels of control, strictness, affection, and communication. This is common when parents are divorced, but also occurs when parents are physically present, yet "absent" because they do not give their children the attention they need.

These parents excessively rely on other caregivers or screens for childcare, using their own selfish activities as an excuse.

Children of such parents tend to have low self-esteem, feel insecure, and do not usually perform well in school.

- **Loving and Firm Parents**

They have good communication, are affectionate with their children, and maintain a high level of control and discipline.

These parents show an excellent balance between being strict and permissive. They set clear limits and enforce them while also expressing their love and sharing emotions with their children.

The children of these parents grow up happy, show great self-control, respect others, and build good relationships. They develop confidence in themselves without becoming arrogant.

THE IMPORTANCE OF CLEAR RULES

Clear rules are fundamental for children.

Just as open communication between parents and children is an indicator of healthy and strong families, it is also important for mom and dad to have good and regular communication with each other. To be successful in raising and disciplining their children, parents must establish together the culture of correction and discipline they will implement at home.

This is not always easy. You and your spouse come from different households with different parenting methods, and sometimes these may even be opposing. One may come from a very strict household while the other from a relaxed one with little discipline.

Regardless of past experiences, parents must determine what is healthy and effective for disciplining their children in their current family. The key to a good discipline culture is communication that leads to parental agreement. Children are left confused when there is no order at home, and when parents contradict or undermine each other. This creates a terrible precedent and should be avoided at all costs.

Clear rules are fundamental for children.

Once parents use good communication to establish how they will parent, they should communicate it with children. Children need to know their responsibilities, what is allowed and what is not. This helps them clearly understand their limits, such as: no hitting others, no yelling, no slamming doors, and responding respectfully with "Yes, ma'am/sir."

THE IMPORTANCE OF SETTING HEALTHY LIMITS

Some key characteristics of children raised with clear and healthy boundaries are:

- They tend to show self-respect.
- They are happier and calmer because they have learned self-control.
- Their world is safer because they function within those limits.
- They have open communication with their parents and trust them.

Below are some ideas that can serve as a model when discussing household rules with your spouse.

Regarding Obedience:

- It must be immediate. Instructions should be followed when given, not when the child decides to.
- When parents give an instruction, children should respond with: "Yes, ma'am/sir" or "Yes, dad/mom."
- Responses like "That's not fair" or expressions of frustration should not be accepted.
- Once parents say "No," children should not keep insisting: "Please, please, please!"

Regarding Responsibilities:

- Everyone must maintain personal hygiene (brushing teeth, bathing, combing hair, etc.).
- Everyone must leave for school on time.
- When returning from school, children must put away their school items and lunch containers in the kitchen.

CONSEQUENCES

As mentioned before, for discipline to work at home, consequences for misbehavior, failure to meet responsibilities, or breaking rules must be clearly established in advance.

A common method is to impose a loss of privileges for each "infraction." Some possible privilege losses for children include:

- No watching TV
- No playing their favorite video game
- No playing outside with friends
- No playing with their toys

Many parents resort to physical punishment for all kinds of misconduct, and Christian parents often justify it with certain scriptures. Some Christian parents even carry a "rod" everywhere.

To begin with, most of the rods I've seen in Christian stores are actually the wooden sticks used to stir 5-gallon paint buckets. They are painted in colors, pink or blue, and they add the inscription: "Son, because I love you I discipline you." However, no matter how pretty they are decorated, for children they are not nice, and they are also not flexible at all, as they are supposed to be for rods.

But let's go to the Bible. Physical punishment, or the use of the rod, is found in the book of Proverbs. It appears mentioned several times, perhaps one of the most well-known verses being the following:

"Whoever spares the rod hates their children, but the one who loves their children is careful to discipline them." (Proverbs 13:24, NIV)

In some verses, it says that the rod is "for the backs of fools" and that it "will drive folly far away from the child." Other versions also use the word "fool" to refer to a senseless person. In this context, rebellion and foolishness are terms used to designate wrong behaviors or attitudes that are observed repeatedly, intentionally, with persistence in doing wrong, open defiance, or intentional challenge to authority.

As we see, not all cases of "disobedience" or "misbehavior" in children would fall into this category.

We might think, then, that this type of correction is necessary but should never be the only one, nor should we use it too frequently.

It has been said that the rod is most effective during the preschool years, but less so as children grow. However, I believe that it is during this stage that it has been used most unjustly, because many times we label an attitude as "rebellious" (especially when the child is two or three years old), when in reality, at the stage of mental development they are in, what is happening is simply that the child does not remember the instruction given. On the other hand, if the disobedience is deliberate—that is, you have just given the instruction and the child insists on doing the wrong thing—then in those cases, the rod often works very well, and even many times it works like a "magic rod": just seeing it, their attitude changes instantly.

In general terms, a great piece of advice for applying the rod or any type of physical correction is never to do it in anger. In addition, it must be clearly established beforehand—for us and for them—when or in what circumstances we will give them physical correction. This must be defined as the Bible frames it: the rod is used to correct rebellion, especially if the child openly defies their parents.

Be very careful, mom! When we misuse this type of discipline, we end up with great feelings of guilt, and we also damage our children's hearts.

Below I present some guidelines and advice so that you can move forward with healthy discipline with your children. If you want to learn more about this topic, I would like to recommend the material by Spanish Christian psychologist David Solá. His book Educate Without Mistreating presents very valuable information about the topic of correction tools for our children.

DO NOT ABUSE OR MISTREAT YOUR CHILD

Parents must be very careful never to abuse their children emotionally, physically, or verbally in the name of discipline. Even if unintentional, anger and frustration can lead to actions or words that damage children's self-esteem.

Modern laws protect children physically. If an adult crosses the line, legal consequences may follow. Even when your actions are legal, it is important for parents to examine their own level of anger or frustration before disciplining their children. If discipline is carried out in anger, it is very likely to be excessive.

Physical discipline should never include:

- Bruises
- Cuts
- Blows to the head
- Hair pulling
- Punching
- Violent shaking
- Muscle injuries (e.g. twisting an arm)

Before determining how you will respond when children misbehave, as they inevitably will, think about what you want your words or actions to teach them.

Any of these things are considered violence or aggression toward the child.

"Spankings" can leave the skin pink, but it should return to its normal color within a couple of minutes. If the redness lasts much longer than 5 minutes, it is possible the spanking was too harsh.

The same happens with the rod. One day when my daughter was little (perhaps three or four years old), I wanted to test for myself how hard I was punishing her because I didn't want to "go overboard." So, I grabbed the famous rod and hit myself with the same intensity I used on her. When I realized the pain it caused me—even though I was bigger and stronger—I decided to stop using that instrument and returned to the old-fashioned tool that served to stop any tantrum or rebellion: the flip-flop! I found that because it is rubbery and flexible, it caused a more superficial pain that went away faster than the sharp sting from that little wooden stick. A soft ruler or one of those plastic spatulas we use to flip pancakes, among other examples of flexible things, can be good options.

Keep in mind that discipline will also require limits for us, the adults. Make an agreement with yourself, making it clear what words you will never use against your children. Commit yourself not to yell at them, and when you do, apologize. Do not discipline when you are under the effect of intense emotions; instead, wait for some time to cool down your emotions and your head. Finally, before applying a punishment or consequence, evaluate the situation to see if the consequence you are about to apply will truly meet the objective of changing that negative behavior in your child.

The purpose of discipline is to keep your child's soul from evil.

The purpose of discipline is to keep your child's soul from evil.

Remember that the purpose of discipline is not to pass judgment, much less to unload your anger or frustration because your children are not behaving as you would like. The purpose of discipline is to keep your child's soul from evil. Therefore, the goal of applying discipline will be the correction of bad behavior and/or the prevention of harmful habits in the child's life.

AVOID PUBLICLY EMBARRASSING YOUR CHILDREN OR LETTING OTHERS INTERVENE IN THEIR CORRECTION

Even if your child misbehaves in public, be sure to correct them privately. If you do it in public, besides embarrassing them, the result will not be the same because the child will be more concerned about protecting their reputation and avoiding embarrassment in front of others than about the wrongdoing or the lesson you are trying to teach.

Another important aspect of discipline is ensuring that not too many people get involved in the punishment. Sometimes siblings might add more information or make an issue bigger than it actually is. Once you have heard everyone and gathered all the necessary information, ask the others to step back and not interfere in the discipline process. This is about respecting your child. The goal is not to expose or shame them in front of others. We are not in a Roman circus.

Similarly, if the father is handling discipline, do not interfere. Let him complete the process and enforce the correction. The idea is to avoid a situation where it becomes "everyone against one." If you need to add something, wait for the right moment, but remember that you must support the father's correction, not undermine him. After the correction, make sure to talk with your child to confirm that the communication with their father was clear so that they do not repeat the same mistake in the future. Be very careful not to change or question the punishment given by the father, creating an image of "unfairness" because it was too harsh. If you feel the father was too harsh in the correction, make sure to talk to him privately so that he himself can approach the child and either modify or soften the previous punishment.

Additionally, remember to inform your husband about the correction you gave the children and the reasons behind them. This will prevent situations where the children recover privileges you had taken away or gain an advantage when they realize their father is unaware of the matter. Sometimes this happens simply because there was no time to discuss it with your spouse. If your children violate the consequences by taking advantage of the parent's lack of information, I recommend doubling the punishment or consequences to set a precedent that parents act in agreement and will not tolerate such tricks.

DO NOT JUSTIFY YOUR AUTHORITY WITH GOD'S AUTHORITY

I have often heard pastors and Christian counselors say that before physically punishing their children, they told them something like, "I'm doing this because God's Word says so, and because I love God and know that this is good for you." One day, I used the same argument with Victoria after disciplining her. Her response left me stunned, and I immediately realized the terrible mistake I had made. She firmly said, "I don't like God anymore."

I could not believe that something so cruel for a child was in the Bible! Until that moment, Victoria had only heard stories about God's love and power in the Word. How could I explain to a small child about justice and judgment? I felt terrible and realized that saying this was, deep down, a way to excuse myself for exercising my authority. The truth is, we correct and discipline our children because we are their parents, and as such, we have the right and obligation to do so, period. We know that we have God's support and His Word to do so, but we do not have to over-explain or apologize for it.

At that moment, I had to pray and ask the Holy Spirit to guide me so I could explain to Victoria the side of God's love that protects and preserves from harm. After talking with her, and by the grace of the Spirit, she returned to God's Word with the same love and tenderness as before.

IMITATE THE LORD'S DISCIPLINE

When God's Word uses the term "correction" or "discipline," it does not strictly refer to physical punishment. In the Bible, we find several occasions when the Lord corrected or disciplined His people, but He always did so using His attributes, such as truth, justice, and mercy. If the Lord had not been merciful and slow to anger, He would have undoubtedly consumed the rebellious, stubborn, and stiff-necked people He had. However, when I read all the messages the prophets delivered on behalf of the Lord to judge the people, I find a perfect balance in God's correction:

Assuring your child of your unconditional love is the most powerful tool for discipline and correction.

- The Lord reminded them of His Words, what He had asked them to keep.
- The Lord pointed out their faults, giving them an opportunity to repent and change.
- When they persisted in wrongdoing, He warned them of the consequences (discipline) so they would change their hearts.
- The Lord gave them hope. He always showed them the path to restoration, the way back to His heart.

"For I will not contend forever, nor will I always be angry; for the spirit would faint before Me, and the breath of those whom I have made." (Isaiah 57:16, LBLA)

REMEMBER THAT LOVE IS THE MOST IMPORTANT ASPECT OF PARENTING

Assuring your child of your unconditional love is the most powerful tool for discipline and correction. It is not fear that will transform their heart. Fear only changes external actions and distances children from their parents. It is firm love that motivates them toward a healthy life and wise decisions.

Take a moment and reflect on this: We are a reflection of God for our children. How often do you remind them that they can always return to you—when they do good and even when they do wrong? How much grace and mercy do you extend to them? Let your love and forgiveness not be some secret code they struggle to interpret. Discuss this with your spouse and agree to openly showing love to your children.

We set boundaries for our children so they are safe and develop in healthy ways, but we must never limit our expressions of love toward them. Nothing makes children feel safer than words of love and affirmation. Hug and kiss them as soon as possible after discipline. Give them time to reflect on their actions but also create quick opportunities for reconciliation. If you apply the biblical principle "Do not let the sun go down while you are still angry" (Ephesians 4:26), you will teach them a lifelong lesson about not holding resentment. This affirms in their hearts that your love for them is unconditional.

Chapter 07

HOW TO HELP YOUR CHILD DEVELOP A HEALTHY SEXUALITY

It is no secret that our world today is facing a great crisis due to a hedonistic and distorted view of sexuality. The major scourges of society, such as human trafficking, pornography, and sexually transmitted diseases, among others, reflect the broken sexuality that afflicts human beings.

Teaching our children about sexuality is teaching them about their essence and identity.

All people were created by God as sexual beings. Teaching our children about sexuality does not mean only talking to them about the sexual act itself. That is just one aspect. Teaching them about sexuality means talking to them about their essence and their identity.

Sex is so inherent to human beings that the first question we ask about a newborn is: “Is it a boy or a girl?” And although some groups today try to claim that a person’s sex is not determined by their genitals but rather by how they “feel” in the future, the truth is that we are not only defined as male or female by our genitals at birth. Every cell in our body carries this information in our genetic code, and it remains that way in our DNA for the rest of our lives.

One time, we bought a pair of Australian parakeets, and the veterinary assistant told us: “You’re taking two females, but this can change.” I was intrigued by her comment and asked her to explain. She clarified that since we cannot see the reproductive organs of these birds, humans differentiate their sex by the color of their beaks. In the case of these parakeets, if the area around the nostrils is blue, it is a male, and if it is ivory, it is a female. However, as they grow, the color of their beak may change until it reaches a final color that reveals their true biological sex. In short, what changes is not the bird’s sex but rather the external reference we use to identify it.

Humans, unlike animals, do not live out their sexuality based purely on instinct. Our sexuality is more complex and involves how we perceive ourselves as men or women, how we interact with others, how we accept our bodies, and how we care for them.

Sexuality is shaped from early childhood. Therefore, it is crucial to properly educate our children during their process of defining and forming their sexuality. We cannot leave this topic up to chance or delegate the responsibility of educating them on this matter to others. We must have a clear goal and purpose in teaching our children about sexuality, ensuring they understand, accept, and fully value their sexuality.

MYTHS ABOUT SEX AND SEXUALITY

If sexuality is not just about being male or female, nor just about reproduction, then what is it and what does it involve? We can define sexuality as the combination of anatomical, physiological, and psychological conditions that characterize each sex. Depending on the culture you are in, there may be different myths or beliefs about sexuality that shape the “desirable” characteristics or behaviors of men and women.

For example, it is often said that men are "real men" when they use their physical strength, have power and money, and do not cry. Likewise, women are considered "real women" when they can meet the emotional, sexual, and physiological needs of men. In some cultures, it is also believed that men are more valuable or important than women.

Unfortunately, mothers have played a key role in perpetuating these myths within the home. By making strong distinctions between boys and girls–whether by giving them different privileges or simply by the things they tell each one–mothers pass down their culture's ideas about how men and women "should be" or what they "should do."

As Christians, we must adopt the culture of God's kingdom, which Jesus Christ came to establish. This is a kingdom where men and women are of equal value before God and must treat each other with mutual respect. Each has specific roles and responsibilities, yes, but these should be defined by the couple based on their culture and unique situation. Regardless, the mutual relationship between a Christian couple should always be based on the model of Christ and His church–a relationship of devotion, love, and honor.

As Christians, we must adopt the culture of the kingdom of God that Jesus Christ came to establish.

The Bible teaches that raising children is a responsibility shared by both parents. Each parent contributes to their children's identity and helps them develop proper ways to relate to themselves, to people of the same sex, and to the opposite sex.

Dr. Meg Meeker, a pediatrician and psychologist, provides valuable insight in her books *Strong Fathers, Strong Daughters* and *Strong Fathers, Strong Sons.* She warns parents, especially fathers, that their presence is vital in raising their children, especially in matters of sexuality. Mothers sometimes make the mistake of isolating fathers from the task of correcting or instructing children, but in God's design, each parent contributes uniquely and significantly to both their daughters and sons.

I firmly believe that the current crisis of sexuality stems from two main factors: the lack of parental involvement in child-rearing and the absence of a consistent and conscious effort by parents to properly educate their children about all aspects of their sexual development.

Many parents avoid or delay discussing these topics with their children due to certain myths they have believed—such as thinking that discussing sexuality is shameful, that talking about it might "ruin" their child's innocence (so it's better to stick to the story of the stork), or that addressing these issues might awaken their child's sexual curiosity too soon.

However, research shows otherwise. A study conducted at the University of Michigan found that 9 out of 10 teenagers said it would be easier for them to delay sexual activity and prevent unwanted pregnancies if they had "open and honest conversations" about these topics with their parents. There is nothing healthier or more natural than for us, as parents, to be the ones who help our children discover God's purpose in creating and teach them how to navigate their sexuality.

THE NORMAL DEVELOPMENT OF SEXUALITY

It is important to understand that children naturally discover their sexuality through observation, exploration, and asking questions. Understanding the normal sexual behaviors that correspond to each age group will help us avoid unnecessary alarm, punishment, or repression. Instead, it allows us to approach them with accurate information so they can understand themselves and treat their bodies appropriately.

Knowing this information also enables parents, doctors, psychologists, and educators to detect potential issues or underlying situations in a child's life and intervene correctly and in a timely manner.

A table compiled by health organizations, available to the public, outlines common sexual behaviors in children at different ages.

Sexual Behaviors Common In Infancy	
Preschool Children (under 4 years old)	Exploring and touching their private parts, in public and private rubbing their genitals (with their hands or objects) show their private parts to others looking when others are naked (in the bathroom, or undressing) talking to other children their age about bodily functions (e.g "peeing" or "pooping")
Young Children (4-6 years old)	Touching their private parts on purpose (masturbating), occasionally in the presence of others Trying to look at others while they're naked or changing Imitating couple behaviors (kissing, holding hands) Exploring the private parts of other children of their age. (E.g playing "doctor" and "if I show you, you show me")

School Age Children (7-12 years old)	Touching themselves on purpose (masturbation), usually in private Playing games with children of the same age that include sexual behaviors (E.g "truth or dare", "family", and "boyfriend-girlfriend") Trying to see other people as they change or are naked Wanting more privacy, like not wanting to change in front of others, or not wanting to talk about sexual themes with adults Starting to feel sexual attraction and interest in other children of their age

However, some childhood sexual behaviors indicate more than simple curiosity and are considered sexual behavior problems. Sexual behavior problems can put at risk the safety and well-being of your child and other children as well. Sexual behavior problems include any act that:

- Is clearly beyond the child's developmental level (for example, a three-year-old trying to kiss an adult's genitals).
- Includes threats, struggling, or aggression.
- Involves children with a wide range of ages (for example, a twelve-year-old "playing doctor" with a four-year-old).
- Produces strong emotional reactions in the child, such as anger (rage, fury) or anxiety.

HOW TO RESPOND TO NORMAL SEXUAL BEHAVIORS AT EACH AGE

When we observe some of the behaviors described in the table, we might feel uneasy and not know how to talk to our children. However, this is an opportunity to assess what they already know and educate them.

For example, if we catch our child touching or stimulating their genitals, we may instinctively react by scolding them: "That's not allowed!" However, this only encourages them to do it secretly and feel guilty afterward.

Before reacting, ask yourself why they do it. If they are young (under four years old), they may do it because it feels pleasant or ticklish. Experts recommend redirecting their focus rather than scolding them.

For older children, we can say: "Those are private parts; don't get used to touching them often because you might do it in public without realizing it." We should also explain that these areas are very sensitive and may cause ticklish sensations, but they must be treated with care for hygiene and health reasons. If the behavior becomes compulsive, it may indicate emotional issues such as fear, insecurity, or anxiety. Instead of just correcting the behavior, we must address the root cause.

When we talk with our children about sexual topics (for example, after noticing in them some behaviors like the ones mentioned in the table), it is important to maintain a calm and steady tone of voice, and whenever possible ask open-ended questions that can help the child feel confident enough to talk with us about this subject. We use open-ended questions so that the child can tell us what happened or what they felt in their own words, rather than just answering "yes" or "no." For example, you could ask your child:

- What were you doing?
- Where did you get the idea?
- How did you learn this?
- How did you feel when you did it?

It is likely that the child simply felt curious, or was playing but was not affected or feeling bad about what they were doing. If you find a situation in which your child feels a little embarrassed, but not disturbed or affected in any other way, this can be an ideal opportunity to talk with them about healthy boundaries and rules regarding sexual behavior.

SEX EDUCATION FOR CHILDREN

Each parent must find out when is the right time to begin a basic dialogue about sexuality with their child. Generally, their questions will indicate to us when it is time to start these conversations. However, there may be cases of children who are not curious enough to ask, but who,

because of the easy access they have to the Internet and television, are informed about these topics – and not in the best way.

This is why sometimes we must take the initiative with them. We cannot keep them in a bubble for long: they go to school, watch television, and have access to our cell phones. Even if we have "security controls," sometimes during "family time" on television, commercials appear with explicit adult sexual activities. This also happens on children's television channels.

On the other hand, even from a very young age, children show curiosity about the human body, the birth of babies, and romantic relationships. It is wonderful to hear the things they are capable of asking, but sometimes they catch us off guard. Questions like: "How are babies born?" or "How did the baby get into mommy's tummy?" should have appropriate answers for each age.

WHAT TO TALK ABOUT AND WHEN?

Whenever you talk to your children about these topics, do so with clarity and truth.

Whenever you talk to your children about these topics, do so with clarity and truth.

We must always answer their questions clearly and appropriately for their age without filling their heads with fantasies or misinformation.

The right time to talk about sex and related topics is a common concern for parents. Some delay these discussions, only to later realize their children already know much more than they thought. With easy access to the internet and television, children are being exposed to these topics, often in the wrong way. That is why we must get ahead of them and guide them with the right information. And what exactly should you talk about at each age? Below, I will share a guide that I found very helpful:

WHAT TO TALK ABOUT WITH CHILDREN UNDER 4 YEARS OLD:

- We should teach them that boys and girls are different, not just because they wear bows or dress differently, but because they are physically different.
- When they ask direct questions about how babies are born, we can give them a true but simple answer: "When the baby has finished forming inside mommy, we go to the hospital, and there, with the help of doctors, the baby is born."

- We should teach them from a young age the correct names for their genitals ("penis" and "vulva") because this will help them see these body parts as just another part of their body, without negative or vulgar connotations. We can also teach them that when we are in public, they can refer to their genitals as "private parts."
- It is necessary to explain to them that there are rules regarding personal boundaries (for example, we must keep private parts covered and not touch other children's private parts, and no one should touch their private parts).

Teaching the child that the response to any threat against their body or privacy is NO gives them security and power.

Through a book we read with Victoria titled *Red Flags*, we taught her that her private parts are those covered by a two-piece swimsuit. These parts cannot be seen or touched by ANYONE, except her parents or a doctor in the presence of one of her parents. If someone asks to see them, that is a "red flag," and she must answer "NO." Likewise, no one can show her their private parts or ask her to touch them. That is also a "red flag," and she must say "NO." Furthermore, all the red flags she perceives should be shared with mom and dad without fear. Remind your child that even if they didn't say no, for any reason, they can always talk with you and they are not in trouble.

Teaching the child that the response to any threat against their body or privacy is NO gives them security and power.

Teaching a child that their response to any threat against their body or privacy is NO gives them security and power. When they do not feel safe or comfortable with someone's request or in a particular situation, they should have the freedom to say NO and feel safe coming to talk to us.

Of course, it is not enough to read a book to a child once. This conversation should be repeated as they grow. We must be aware that most cases of sexual abuse occur with "trusted" people close to the family and home. Therefore, we must be smart, be careful about what we expose our children to, and give them the confidence that they can come to us in any situation.

WHAT TO TALK ABOUT WITH YOUNG CHILDREN (BETWEEN 4 AND 6 YEARS OLD):

- We must teach them that boys' and girls' bodies change over the years.
- We should give them simple explanations about how babies grow inside mothers' wombs and the birth process. We can provide them with technical information about how the body works: "God gave each woman a special place where babies grow. It is not the stomach because that is only for food. It is another pouch called the uterus. When the baby is fully formed and ready to be born, mommy's muscles work to push and help the baby out. The baby comes out through a special passage designed by God for that purpose, which is called the vagina."
- It is important to explain that they might feel a pleasant sensation when they touch their private parts, but this is something they should do in private.
- We must continue reinforcing the rules regarding personal boundaries (such as keeping private parts covered and not touching other children's private parts). Additionally, we must emphasize that if someone touches them inappropriately, it is NEVER their fault, and they should immediately go to mom or dad.

Here, we can introduce topics like modesty. Personally, I like to define it as being careful about not showing one's private parts. Others define modesty as the shame of exposing what is private, but to me, feelings like shame can fade as we become accustomed to a situation or begin to see it as normal. However, when I adopt an attitude of care or concern for my body, I am setting a boundary and defining how to protect my privacy. Modesty also involves being reserved or cautious in how we speak and what we talk about, as well as being careful in how we dress and behave socially.

This is also a good age to start educating our children about self-esteem and physical beauty. Between the ages of three and four, children begin to recognize themselves as boys or girls. In the case of girls, it is normal for them to want to wear dresses, have long hair, and use makeup. It is also normal for both boys and girls to associate personal care (such as bathing, combing their hair properly, or dressing well) with beauty. At the same time, we often say: "How handsome!" or "How beautiful you look!" to encourage proper self-care.

As moms, we must help our children from a young age to identify what behaviors are appropriate and which are not.

However, we must be careful when beauty turns into competition ("I have to be the prettiest") or when beauty involves pain or lack of mobility ("I don't play to avoid getting dirty" or "to avoid messing up my hair"). (We moms know that the pain of beauty will come later... so why make them suffer early!)

Another thing we must be careful about is emphasizing their own beauty and not encouraging them to imitate or chase after the sexual symbols of the moment that appear on TV or in video games. Young children cannot distinguish between good and bad. They imitate everything: behavior, movements, and culture. We must be there to tell them, "No, honey, we don't do that," or to correct whatever is necessary.

One time, my daughter was invited to a birthday party. All the girls were around seven or eight years old. There was loud music playing, and what surprised me the most was a little girl who not only knew the lyrics to all the songs but also all the dance moves. It was like watching MTV live! What shocked me was the surprised look on her mother's face. She was just as astonished as I was! Later, I saw the mother asking how she knew all the songs. "My daddy," the girl answered. Then I understood the situation: The parents were divorced, and while her dad took care of her, that was what she watched.

As moms, we must help our children from a young age to identify what behaviors are appropriate and which are not.

When our children imitate pop culture it will sometimes seem funny. As moms, we must help them recognize which behaviors are appropriate and which are not, even if they are popular.

WHAT TO TALK ABOUT WITH SCHOOL-AGE CHILDREN (BETWEEN 7 AND 12 YEARS OLD):

- We must provide them with basic information about reproduction, pregnancy, and childbirth.
- We must teach them about the consequences and risks associated with sexual activity (such as pregnancy or sexually transmitted diseases). By this age, they likely already know of someone who became pregnant without being married or a similar case.
- This is a good time to teach them that intimacy is not something to be shared lightly with just anyone and that we should wait for the appropriate age to start romantic relationships. Sexual relationships should be within a committed and exclusive relationship, which we call marriage.

- From the age of 10, we should teach them what to expect and how to handle the changes that puberty will bring (including menstruation and wet dreams).

During this stage, we will also have to answer some very common questions such as: "Why do people kiss?", or "When they kiss, do they have a baby?". These are questions that can open the door for us to teach them about healthy expressions or demonstrations of affection. Some answers could be:

"When people know each other very well in friendship, other stronger feelings are born that go beyond just being friends; that's when love is born and the desire to spend more time together."

"When a man and a woman feel love, there are special and exclusive ways of treating each other only for that person, like holding hands, hugging, and kissing. This is not something we do when we are friends or when we are little; these relationships happen when we are older."

"After a period of getting to know each other, which we call dating, people decide to make a bigger commitment called marriage. Then they go live together to form a family and wait there for their babies."

BUT THEN, HOW DO BABIES GET THERE?

This is a question that children may ask us from a very young age, and you can give them a simple answer without details. Something like: "Babies are a gift from God that He gives to parents when they love each other very much."

Later on, during the school years, and once they clearly understand how babies are born, it will be time to teach them about conception. If they still haven't asked the question: "How do babies get there?", then you will need to be the one to bring up the topic. One good way to do this is by saying: "You know how babies are born, but do you know how God's design works so that a baby can exist in the mother's womb?"

Another way to introduce the topic is through the tools we have today. For example, through television programs or educational videos. With my daughter, we started the topic after watching an episode of "The Magic School Bus." There, they talked about the difference between an unfertilized egg and the "rooster-hen" egg, which is where chicks come from. The question was: "Why, if all eggs look the same, don't they all hatch chicks?" And her answer was: "Because for there to be a chick, the egg must have the dad's part too."

"Well," I told her, "that's how all animals are formed, and humans too! We all have a part from mom and a part from dad. The way the parts are joined or fertilized can vary between animals and humans.

In humans, the egg, called the 'ovum,' is inside the mother, well protected. The part the father contributes for a baby to be born is called the 'sperm,' which is also inside him and comes out through his penis. For the mother's egg to meet the father's part, mom and dad need to unite. How do they unite? Dad places his penis inside mom, and that way makes sure his sperm reaches where mom's egg is waiting. After that, mom keeps this union, which is first called an 'embryo,' in her womb, and later, when it grows, it's called a 'baby.'"

As you can see, the explanation is purely technical and sounds like something from a science class. But unlike in class, we mothers can add to the explanation the elements of joy and love that surround this miracle of life.

HOW TO PROTECT OUR CHILDREN FROM PORNOGRAPHY

Sadly, nowadays pornography is no longer a topic exclusive to adults, or even to young people. Dr. Josh McDowell, along with other leaders in various fields who research the subject, warns that the average age at which children are entering the world of pornography is eight years old.

The reason this age has dropped so much is the easy access to the Internet that our children have. If we do not address this in time and in the right way, the damage can be devastating for our little ones. Also, keep in mind that pornography is not an exclusively male issue: statistics now show that the number of women consuming pornography is almost equal to that of men.

But where does it all start? Most children begin consuming pornography by accident (because they stumbled upon a website, or someone showed it to them), for fun, or out of curiosity. The problem is that once they find it, they get hooked, because it works in the brain the same way a drug does, and it produces the same result: satisfaction. For this reason, even if they want to quit, sooner or later they will realize they cannot do it on their own.

A child's brain cannot control the impulses that pornography stimulates, making them more prone to fall into an addiction.

A child's brain cannot control the impulses that pornography stimulates, making them more prone to fall into an addiction.

A child's brain cannot control the impulses that pornography stimulates, making them more prone to fall into an addiction that is harder to break than drugs or alcohol. In addition, a child's brain is more vulnerable to pornography because it is designed to imitate what it sees.

Why is pornography so addictive? Because it produces sensations of arousal in the body, which our brain responds to with visual stimuli by releasing chemicals that bring pleasure, but only for a short time.

At this point, we must understand that there are two parts of our brain involved when it comes to creating an addiction: the feeling brain and the thinking brain. The feeling brain has to do with the systems that help us survive, such as feeling hunger, cold, thirst, or the need to go to the bathroom. When the brain alerts us to these needs and we meet them, it rewards us with feelings of satisfaction. The issue is that this part of the brain does not discern whether the need is good or bad; it only detects it. This is precisely where the deception of pornography lies: although it generates a pleasant sensation, in the end, it leaves us with emotions like loneliness, shame, and guilt. (Feelings that also lead to isolation from what is beneficial.) The main damage caused by pornography is that it distorts God's divine purpose for sex as a means of expression between a man and a woman within marriage. And yes, the fantasies it generates can eventually incapacitate people from establishing a long-term romantic relationship with a real human being.

HOW TO TALK TO OUR CHILDREN ABOUT PORNOGRAPHY?

Here are some valuable tips I'd like to share with you:

1. Always speak to them with truth and clarity

To be able to do this, you first need to remove from yourself any kind of shame, morbid curiosity, or "religiosity" regarding the topic. Then, when you talk to your children, use good terms and clear definitions, such as: "Pornography is images, videos, or even cartoons of people with little or no clothing. They focus on those parts of our body that are private, the ones we usually cover with a swimsuit." Explain to them that just as there are good photos and videos that evoke nice moments and healthy things, there are also bad photos and videos that show things that are not good to see; those images are pornography.

A more complete definition for the more mature child could be something like: "When we talk about pornography, we mean material designed to generate sexual feelings in people through their nudity or sexual conduct. There you will find images, stories, sounds, symbols, actions, and words that refer to sexual conduct."

2. Include feelings in your conversations about pornography

When a child, or really any person, looks at pornography, they experience mixed feelings–conflicting feelings. On one hand, they may feel like they want to see more, and on the other, they feel like they don't want to. Children need to know that it's normal for our body to react to these images with various kinds of feelings, even with opposite feelings that appear mixed, such as:

I don't want to see	I want to see more
I feel disgusted	I feel curious
I feel it's wrong	I feel it's good
It makes me feel bad	I'm attracted to it
I feel ashamed	It seems interesting

We also need to explain to them that the feeling that will last the longest is guilt. And the only way to be free from this guilt is to tell their parents about it, because talking about it takes away its power and secrecy. Of course, parents should also pray with them and ask the Lord to free and cleanse them from this feeling.

It has been amazing how some parents in our church have experienced great openness from their children when they bring up these topics. In some cases, thanks to God, the conversations have happened in time, and parents have been able to pray for their little ones and restore that innocence the enemy had stolen from them.

3. Give your child practical advice on what to do if they are tempted or exposed to pornography

Pornography is actually a type of sexual abuse, as it exposes the child to feelings they are not yet ready to handle. Therefore, as a mother, you should teach them what to do when faced with any kind of pornographic material. Some tips you can give them are:

- Close your eyes immediately and walk away!
- Tell a trusted adult as soon as possible.
- Call what you saw by its name: pornography. Identifying it will help your brain and conscience to reject it.
- When you feel the temptation to search for pornography again, distract your mind. Do something positive or something that interests you more (like exercising, playing a game, etc.).

Finally, mom, make sure you empower your child. Tell them confidently: "I know that in any situation, you will always be able to make the best decision!"

OTHER WAYS TO PROTECT OUR CHILDREN

- **Protecting all devices they have access to**
  Let's make sure to ask for help from someone who knows how to set up systems or applications in our homes that block "adult content" on all devices that have access to the internet.

- **Having control over where, when, and how much**
  Today we can't be too careful, since there is no type of safeguard in commercials that appear on television or YouTube, even if the programs being watched are "family-friendly." The content of commercials, whether for products or for other shows aired on the same channel, often includes images and behaviors that are not appropriate for young viewers.

Let's follow the advice of experts and not allow our children to have computers or televisions in their rooms. The issue is more challenging with iPads and cell phones, but by setting clear rules for their use, we can protect what our children see.

I say "clear rules" because most parents do not communicate the "rules of the game" before it begins. Before handing them a video game or allowing them to download an app, you should research it. If you don't have much information, then you should take the time to watch the program or play the game with them before leaving them alone in front of the screens.

Also set limits on when and where they can use each device. It's recommended that at night devices such as phones, iPads, etc., be charged outside of the bedrooms where we sleep. This not only limits access during the hours when children should be resting but also prevents them from being exposed to so much radiation for so long. In other words, it will serve as a time to "detox" from the waves these devices emit.

WHAT DO I DO IF I DISCOVER MY CHILD IS WATCHING PORNOGRAPHY?

God created us with a moldable mind that can be renewed when we choose new paths.

As I said before, it's very important to understand that your child is being a victim of sexual abuse. Don't make the mistake of yelling at them, shaming them, or accusing them for this. Don't use offensive or hurtful words like "You're disgusting!" or "You're perverted for watching that stuff!" Be very careful with your words so as not to add more guilt or shame to what they already feel.

Of course, you should talk about these topics with your child in a private setting, so as not to expose them. You should repeat to them once again what pornography is and what its effect on the brain is. Then you should allow them a space where they can talk about what they feel or ask any questions they might have. Finally, pray with them and ask God to help them be free, and to remove their guilt and shame.

If you see that it's truly a strong addiction problem, seek the advice of professionals in the field so you can better help your child.

God created us with a moldable mind that can be renewed when we choose new paths.

The hope in all these situations is that our brain is capable of creating new, healthy connections. That's right! God created us with a moldable mind that can be renewed when we choose new paths. What wonderful news!

Chapter 08

THE ADDICTIVE POWER OF ELECTRONIC DEVICES

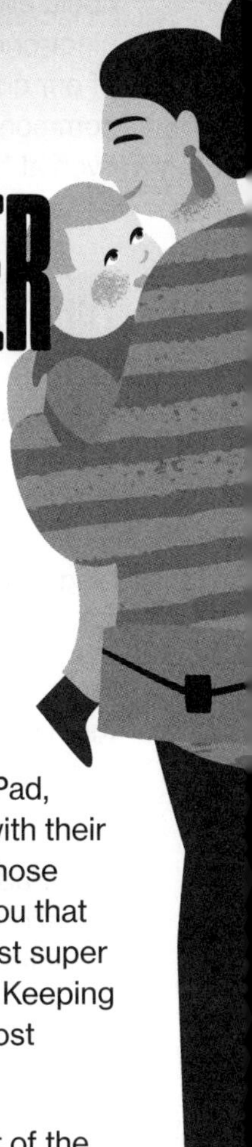

Since smartphones were invented and Mac created the iPad, families have been able to go to restaurants more often with their young children... If you listen to the stories of parents of those who are now teenagers or young adults, they will all tell you that when their children were little, it was impossible (or at least super stressful) to go to a restaurant or go shopping with them. Keeping them still at the table without getting restless was an almost impossible mission.

In Latin America, nannies, nanas, and babysitters are part of the family, and are almost indispensable to working parents. While the nannies take care of the children at home, the adults can do their work and have a social life in peace. But in the United States, having a full-time nanny is not as feasible. Very few people can afford one for even a few hours a week. Before technology flooded the market, families simply deprived themselves for a few years of going to restaurants, movies, and other social activities due to the challenges of going out with little ones.

Nowadays, babies and children of all ages can be "calm" (one could even say "absent") for long periods thanks to the use of electronic devices. These devices have become the babysitters of our children and the tranquilizers for temper tantrums. It is very common to see children in cars, airports, churches, strollers, and even at home quiet and calm, immersed in these devices.

THE BIG LEAP TO TECHNOLOGY: THE IPAD

Before April 2010, cell phones were already tempting children, but their screens were too small for their little fingers to easily interact with the device. Additionally, parents could easily hide phones in their pockets or purses. Then the iPad appeared: bigger and brighter. Plus, thanks to their protective cases, the whole family could use them, even little destroyers.

Touchscreen technology is so easy for little ones to use many of them now approach modern TV screens and try to do the same. (Understanding how a remote control works takes them a couple more years!)

The iPad quickly captured the world's attention, especially the attention of the youngest ones. They can spend many hours a day interacting with iPads, watching endless videos that seem to provoke a "zombie effect" in them.

Although these devices greatly help parents' "peace" and "mental health," and despite the fact that educational apps promise to enhance children's learning, studies have begun to show how these devices are modifying children's brains, negatively affecting their emotional health and even their physical development.

"DO EDUCATIONAL GAMES ON ELECTRONIC DEVICES MAKE CHILDREN SMARTER?" MYTH OR TRUTH?

Although almost all children's apps are marketed as tools to make children smarter and prevent learning difficulties in school, this is not entirely true. Educational applications are created with the intention of helping children learn in a fun way. In that, they are right: Fun does facilitate children's learning. But many studies are now showing that "the cure is worse than the disease." As parents, we must analyze what other options we have to ensure that our children develop their intellectual capacity.

The excessive use of technology has made children dumber.

Electronic devices are not perfect solutions. No studies prove that an iPad can make a preschooler smarter or teach them to speak other languages. What it can do is turn your child into an "expert" in the apps they use most. Here, it's worth remembering that intelligence is not just knowing certain things. Intelligence—or IQ—is a set of skills. In school, children are typically evaluated in seven areas: language, information, memory, mathematics, spatial intelligence, logical reasoning, and fine motor skills.

We should not deceive ourselves into thinking that putting children in front of screens is helping them. What we should do as parents is help our children develop comprehensively. At the end of this chapter, I will give you a guide with ideas to help your children develop all areas of their intelligence.

In 2017, experienced teachers Joe Clement and Matt Miles published a book that had a huge impact on thousands of parents in the United States. In the book, *Screen Schooled*, they explain how excessive use of technology has made children dumber. Based on their vast experience in different educational environments, Clement and Miles argue that rather than stimulating children's learning, using these devices makes it harder for them to focus and leads to them being more easily distracted. It seems that the solution to today's children's learning problems is not giving them more screens, but minimizing their screen time as much as possible.

IF "EDUCATIONAL APPS" ARE SO GREAT, WHY DON'T THEIR OWN CREATORS LET THEIR CHILDREN USE THEM?

A few years ago, an article appeared in a magazine that my husband and I read. The author of the article had attended a children's app developers' convention in 2013. There, a few dozen creators had gathered to showcase the latest applications and games. Most of them were well aware of children's interests from 18 months to 4 years old, so the apps revolved around assembling simple puzzles, building towers with blocks only to destroy them, recognizing letter sounds, etc. Among the creators was a former teacher of the renowned Montessori learning method who was also a mother of four. She had created an app to teach children letter sounds. The journalist asked her, "What games do your children like?", "Oh no, they don't play games like these much," the woman replied. Surprised by the response, the journalist asked why that was the case. The woman replied, "Because we don't allow them. They are prohibited from using electronic devices during the week, unless strictly required by school. I only allow them to use them on weekends, and for no more than 30 minutes. I don't want them to become addicted or overly stimulated by them."

Electronic devices have become the babysitters of many children.

Electronic devices have become the babysitters of many children.

Faced with this response, which truly surprised her, the journalist decided to ask other developers what rules they applied for their own children on this topic. One said he only allowed them to use them on airplanes or during long car trips. Another said only on Wednesdays and weekends, and only for half an hour each day.

In 2007, Bill Gates, then president of Microsoft, set a screen time limit when he noticed his daughter developing an addictive behavior toward video games. He also didn't allow his children to have cell phones until they were 14. (In the U.S., the current average age for a child to own a phone is 10 years old.)

Steve Jobs, former creator and president of Apple, revealed in a *New York Times* interview that he forbade his children from using the then newly-launched iPad (created in 2010). "We limit all the technology our children use at home," he told reporter Nick Bilton.

DANGERS AND CONSEQUENCES OF THE INAPPROPRIATE USE OF TECHNOLOGY

The reasons why technology experts don't allow their own children to use them excessively is precisely because they know the power these devices have and do not want their children's brains, which are still developing, to receive stimuli of this type and develop addictive behaviors.

Neuroscience has advanced by leaps and bounds in recent years thanks to the ability science has developed to measure and understand more deeply what happens in the brain, especially in the area of causes and effects. (A stimulus is given to the brain—visual, auditory, or sensory—and the reaction is observed.) One of the newest concepts neuroscience has introduced is the "elasticity" or "plasticity" of the brain. This refers to the structure and connections the brain creates according to a person's behavior and experiences.

It is in our hands, as parents, to decide what type of mental development we want to promote in our children. Electronics will never create the connections our children need, even if their apps are marketed as "educational." So, what's the solution then? Well, just as we seek to give our children a varied and healthy diet, we must also do the same with entertainment. If we don't want to create harmful patterns or habits that we will later have to fix, we need to be intentional about limiting their technology usage time, while also offering them interesting and healthy alternatives to spend their time.

Electronic devices also pose dangers to the emotional health of children and teenagers. There are many studies linking depression in adolescence to excessive screen exposure, especially on social media. That's why it's so important to establish correct habits for them from an early age regarding the use and time spent on these devices. Protecting them in their childhood and teaching them to make good decisions in adulthood is not only our job but also our obligation.

6 TIPS TO HELP YOU LIMIT YOUR CHILDREN'S SCREEN TIME

1. Set the example

Sorry to start with the hardest one, but there's no other way to begin. Children usually repeat the behavior they see modeled by their parents. If they see you reading a book, they'll be more likely to enjoy reading. If they see you spending many hours in front of the TV, they will do the same.

It's very hard to help our children when there are no good habits within the family. But knowing all the benefits of limiting screen time, it's worth the effort!

It's very important that mom and dad agree on this matter and establish the rules that will govern device use at home. Then make sure to follow them, because if you don't, your children will remind you—and not in a pleasant way.

It's your job as a mom to encourage your children to have healthy behaviors and limit those that are not, even if it means making unpopular decisions.

2. Limit the time

If you're not going to completely turn off the TV or other devices, at least set an appropriate time for your children to use them. Time here refers both to the amount and the occasion. For example, you might tell your children they can watch a program or play a video game for 20 minutes, but only after finishing their chores or responsibilities at home.

3. Promote other activities

Provide your children with the necessary resources (books, board games, art supplies) so they have healthy and entertaining alternatives in which to invest their time. Make sure to get involved in some of those games and activities yourself.

The simple fact that you participate will make any proposal more interesting to your children!

In our case, one challenge we had with Victoria was limiting the use of the TV or iPad during the trip to church. It takes us almost an hour to drive there, so she was used to using some device to keep entertained. That meant an hour going and another coming back with Victoria glued to the screen. We realized that not only was this harming her, but we were also missing out on precious time to interact with her. When we told her we had decided to replace it with another activity, she didn't take it well at first. Everything seemed "boring" to her... until we found something that caught her attention: riddles! Over time, we all became experts at them, and now the challenge is to invent them. We're teaching Victoria to be creative, and these are also our moments of most laughter during the week!

4. Play with your children and get involved in their lives

Sit on the floor with your children. Take a doll, a toy car, or a ball, and play with them. Being intentional about showing selfless love when they are between 4 and 10 years old will bear fruit when they turn 13. You'll be glad you did it!

As a family, don't miss out on mealtimes by having a device to distract them. Take advantage of those moments to talk and ask questions. You can also tell them things they don't know about you, and from your childhood. For many parents, it's easier to turn on the TV than to get involved in their children's lives. But those moments of putting everything else aside and dedicating time to them are essential for successful parenting. Observe, listen, ask questions, and participate. That's also part (and a very important part) of your role as a mother.

5. Pay attention to changes in behavior

Devices have a long-term effect, but they can also have an immediate impact on children's behavior. After a lot of television or video games, they can become irritable, aggressive, selfish, and impatient. If you make the effort to replace screens with other activities, even if you're not the most popular mom in the neighborhood, you'll find your children start using their creativity more, playing with more enthusiasm, and feeling happier.

6. No TVs in the bedrooms

No TVs in your children's bedrooms, and not in yours either.

Limiting the time your children spend in front of screens may seem like an impossible task or a tough battle to fight. But it's worth the fight! And if you truly want to do it, you have to start somewhere. Keep in mind that implementing some steps immediately will help you put the others into practice later. Television is a collective impulse habit: the more you do it, the more likely you are to keep doing it. But the opposite is also true—the more you turn it off, the easier it will be to keep it off!

7 TIPS (WITHOUT SCREENS) TO DEVELOP YOUR PRESCHOOLER'S INTELLIGENCE

A few pages ago, I promised to give you a guide with good ideas to help your preschool-aged children develop all areas of their intelligence. Well, here it is. Karen Quinn is a well-known parent coach for preschool children, advising parents to prepare their kids for starting school so they can pass the tests at the most demanding schools in Manhattan, NY. Below are some practical tips from her book Testing for Kindergarten:

- **Talk to your child about anything, ALL THE TIME.** This will help build their language skills. Children raised in environments with a lot of communication score almost 38 points higher on IQ tests than those from homes with little dialogue.

- **Read books with pictures that teach concepts.** Concepts like colors, shapes, seasons, fruits, or farm animals. All basic information is useful for a preschool child.

- **Challenge your child's memory.** After reading a book to your child, ask them to tell the story in their own words. Also, use patterns or sequences they can repeat. These activities will help develop both verbal and visual memory.

- **Include math concepts in your conversations.** "Dinner will be ready in 5 minutes." "Do you want the whole cookie or half?" "What cute little fingers you have, let's count them!" "Oh, I see you have three chocolates. I'm going to give you two more. Now you have five!" You can also include math when reading picture books: "Look how many arms the octopus has! Let's count them!"

- **Provide your child with toys like blocks, puzzles, Legos, etc.** All of these activities develop spatial skills. Books with hidden drawings or objects to find in different settings are also great.

- **Let your child solve problems.** When toys roll under the table or bookshelf, ask them to figure out how to get them. When they can't get dressed in time for school, ask them to find faster ways to do it. Let them think about how to solve their problems; don't solve them or dictate everything. This will help them gain confidence and decision-making skills. Research shows that children who make decisions freely at home develop strong cognitive skills useful outside the home too.

- **Always keep plenty of craft and art supplies available.** On rainy days or when you don't have many plans, let their creativity grow with crayons, child-safe scissors, glue sticks, modeling clay, paintbrushes, and paints. These activities will help develop fine motor skills and hand-eye coordination–and they're also a lot of fun!

- **Bonus: Make play a priority.** Playing is like a vitamin that supports the development of all intelligence skills. If your child enjoys the activities they do, they will see learning as something pleasant and not as an obligation. As a mom, can you think of a better investment of time than this?

Chapter 09

HOW TO PASS ON A SINCERE FAITH TO YOUR CHILD

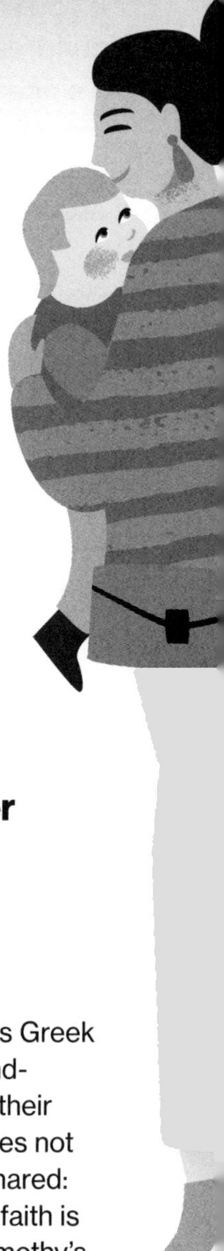

"I am reminded of your sincere faith, which first lived in your grandmother Lois and in your mother Eunice, and I am persuaded that it now lives in you also."
2 Timothy 1:5

Although Timothy came from a home where his father was Greek and his mother was Jewish, it is evident that both his grandmother and his mother did an excellent job of passing on their faith to Timothy. What stands out to me is that the text does not just say "faith," but it specifies the kind of faith that was shared: a "sincere faith." What does Paul mean by this? A sincere faith is a pure faith, without pretense. We are not told whether Timothy's father embraced the same faith, but it is clear practiced their faith both at home and publicly. Theirs was a faith without masks or religiosity—a real faith.

If you want to raise children who have a sincere faith, you must first have a sincere faith yourself.

If you want to raise children who have a sincere faith, you must first have a sincere faith yourself.

Mom, if you want to have children full of faith, the first one who must genuinely embrace this faith is you! In addition, the apostle Paul teaches us that faith must be accompanied by works that are consistent with that faith. The apostle Peter also teaches us in 2 Peter 1:5-8 that in order to grow in faith, we must add certain things:

- Virtue or moral excellence
- Knowledge (a love for knowing the Scriptures and deepening faith concepts)
- Self-control (this speaks of maturity, of not letting ourselves be controlled by other things but rather having the ability to control ourselves)
- Perseverance and constancy
- Submission or devotion to God
- Fraternal affection
- Love

The apostle Peter goes on to say that if we abound in these things, we will not only grow in the knowledge of the Lord Jesus but also become more useful and productive people.

Another great example of a mother who knew how to pass on her sincere faith to her son is Hannah. Her story is told in 1 Samuel, chapter 1.

Hannah conceived Samuel after a transformative experience with God. Discouraged by her barrenness, she had poured out her soul in the temple, pleading with the Lord for a son and promising that if He granted her one, she would dedicate that son to Him.

She meant what she said, because when her child grew to an age where he no longer depended on her, Hannah took him to live at the temple (even though some religious leaders there had no respect for the God they served).

If I had been in Hannah's situation, I think I probably would have explained to the Lord that although dedicating my son to Him had been my initial intention, I was no longer so sure about it because those who would be close to my son there were not the best example of purity and consecration. (Thinking about it, isn't this what our children face daily?)

But that's not what happened with Hannah—and Samuel's story did not end there. Scripture reveals that one day, while the child was living under the care of the priest Eli, something happened: While the priest was sleeping in his room, little Samuel was sleeping in the sanctuary, where the ark of God was. God called Samuel. At first, Samuel thought Eli was calling him, but he eventually realized it was the Lord Himself. Without hesitation, Samuel responded, "Speak, for your servant is listening."

But let me go back a bit to highlight a detail that we sometimes miss. Did you notice where Samuel was sleeping? In the temple of Jehovah, where the ark of God was. The child sought to be close to God's presence day and night! That means he likely remembered his mother's words and her accounts of the God she had known and experienced. Scripture tells us that before his mother took him to live in the temple, she preferred to stay in her city with little Samuel until he was ready to be left there. That is, she dedicated intentional time to preparing young Samuel. And what a great job she did!

In Chapter 1, I mentioned that the window of time we have to invest in and sow into our children what we desire is limited to just a few years. In those early years, we lay the foundations for what their adult life will be. I can imagine how many times Hannah told Samuel about her encounter with God that day in the temple! She even spoke to him about his purpose on this earth when she named him Samuel, which means "God hears." From a very young age, Samuel was the voice of God in the nation of Israel. He always proclaimed that God was not a distant God but one who had ears for those who sought Him genuinely. God used Samuel throughout his life, and in doing so, He honored the faith and work of Samuel's mother.

TRANSFERRING FAITH THROUGH AN EXAMPLE OF FAITH

In his book *Raising Kingdom Kids*, Dr. Tony Evans states that "the simple and greatest reason we are losing our young people is that the home is no longer the place where faith is transferred." The fundamental purpose of parenting at home is evangelism and discipleship of children.

Since I was a child, I have enjoyed sharing the transformative message of the Gospel. Attending a Catholic school and noticing how my friends lived out their faith differently, I set out to convey to them what I believed and show them how it could become real in their lives. This meant I made every effort that during all the years I studied with them, my behavior—both inside school and at birthday parties—was consistent with my message. My greatest message to them for about six years was my own life!

I thank God because the faith I knew and the lifestyle I learned in church were never legalistic or full of messages like, "You can't do this" and "You can't do that," because I believe I wouldn't have been able to live my adolescence otherwise! My faith in Jesus Christ was always sincere and real. I fell in love with the God of the Bible from an early age, and that single truth made my life shine. If I studied, I did my best; if I played sports, I gave it my all; if I did embroidery (yes, my school was run by nuns), I spent hours on it; if I went to birthday parties, I celebrated with joy. All this with a clear conscience, without losing control, and without pretending to be "holier than thou."

What was my motivation? It was the goal I had set. I had already told my classmates that I was going to show them what it meant to be a Christian. I couldn't, nor did I want to, let my words fall flat because of my way of life. My goal was to invite them to know the Lord.

Children are very observant, and they always notice if there are differences between what we say and how we live.

Years after graduation, when technology reconnected us, I got back in touch with many of them. What great satisfaction I felt hearing the testimony of several saying, "Now I am a Christian! I remember when you spoke to me, and I want to say—thank you."

Children are very observant, and they always notice if there are differences between what we say and how we live.

The experience I had in school when I was younger is, in essence, what I must continue practicing at home now that I am a mother. Now I have a pair of little eyes watching me, a pair of ears listening intently to everything I say, and a mind that observes and analyzes my life at every moment. Children are very observant, and they always notice if there are differences between what we say and how we live. They do not do this out of judgment; our children analyze our lives in contrast with our faith simply because that is their learning process. Theory is explained by practice. Practice helps theory be understood and remembered. When theory and practice differ, children do not understand the concept we say is important.

TRANSMITTING THE ESSENTIAL CONCEPTS OF FAITH

As moms, we should take advantage of every moment in daily life to pass on to our children the concepts of faith. Here's a list of ideas that can help you in this purpose.

Forgiveness

A good idea is that when we pray together at night and go over the day, we ask our children if there is something or someone they need to forgive. Then we can help them make Jesus' prayer effective when He said, "Forgive us our sins, for we also forgive everyone who sins against us."

But they also want to see your forgiveness in action. Take advantage of opportunities you have with them, accepting their apologies when they behave rudely or disobediently. And when you correct them and have applied the necessary discipline, be careful not to keep resentment in your heart toward them. Look for ways to promote dialogue and reconciliation, without necessarily removing the consequences for wrong actions. Avoid phrases like: "I'm never going to forgive you for this," and much less apply those "silent treatments" that last for days, which only make it obvious that the sun has gone down on our anger!

Love

Love is the most tangible thing we can teach. We love with words, acts of service, gifts, tender caresses, respect, and many other ways. The most biblical way we can teach this concept is by showing love to our spouses, our children, our neighbors, and even to those who are hard to love.

It's important to emphasize to children that love is not just speaking words of love. Love is always tied to commitment, consistency, and certain actions that prove that love. When we cook for them, let's take the opportunity to say: "I do it gladly, because it's a way of expressing my love to you." (Yes, even if you don't like cooking.) And when we ask them to clean their room or help with housework, let's emphasize that it's a practical way to love the family.

As mothers, we must keep in mind that for a constant love to flow from us, we need to draw near to the source from which perfect love flows—God. Only then will we be able to overcome physical fatigue, the strain of routine, and the small (or big) frustrations of life, and even overlook the ingratitude our children may sometimes show.

Finally, if you can show them love, you must emphasize that God loves them even more, and explain to them that Jesus' motivation for coming into the world was precisely that: His great love for us.

Humility

If there's one thing I've noticed melts our children's hearts, it's when we come to them admitting our mistakes. Surely, at some point we will make an injustice when we discipline them, whether because we didn't believe them or because we didn't have all the facts at hand at the moment of correction. Surely at some point we will "go too far" with punishment, or yell at them–not so much because they deserve it, but because of our own frustration. Surely at some point we will fail in situations where they expected our presence. But there's nothing more reconciling than coming to our children in humility and asking their forgiveness for our mistakes.

Does this make you seem vulnerable? Surely it does. However, because of the results in them and for the good of the relationship, it's worth showing vulnerability in this area.

We cannot model to our children that the Christian life is a perfect life. That is a lie, and if that's what we demand from them, sooner or later they will turn away from everything that has to do with God. The Christian life we should model at home must be a genuine life, in which when we fail or sin, we use humility as the vehicle to be restored by our good and merciful God.

CLARIFYING CONCEPTS ABOUT GOD

When our daughter, Victoria, was about four years old, we encouraged her to lead certain moments of prayer at home, whether at mealtime or at the end of the day. However, we noticed that she constantly refused to do it. I always enjoy hearing the prayers of our friends' children when we share a meal and even how they even argue among siblings about who gets to lead the prayer. But I didn't see this interest in my daughter. Was it perhaps due to a lack of siblings?

One day, after insisting that she lead a prayer, little Victoria responded, "Why do you want me to pray? You keep praying; you do it very well." That helped explain things. We then shared with her that prayer was not about saying the right words but about the fact that God longs to have a personal relationship with each of us, and what mattered most to Mom and Dad was that she would have a friendship with Jesus. From then on, Danilo and I began praying for the Lord to reveal Himself to her, even at her young age. We prayed for Victoria to have an encounter with God and for the concept of God to become real to her.

It didn't take more than a week before Victoria woke up very happy one morning, telling us she'd had a dream. The dream had been very clear. She had seen a big bed with four pillows: one for Dad, one for Mom, one for her, and one for Jesus. Then, she had seen four sinks, one of which belonged to Jesus.

The presence of Jesus had become so real to her following the dream that when mealtime came, she served a fourth plate, placed it on the table, and said, "This one is for Jesus."

After that experience, God stopped being something ethereal, intangible, and invisible for Victoria. She had understood that Jesus was part of her daily life at home, and when she prayed at the table, she looked at the empty seat and knew He was sitting with us. Her way of communicating with God through prayer could not have been more natural!

As parents, we must not assume that our children will easily adopt our faith practices. In our search to understand why Victoria didn't want to pray, she also shared this: "God doesn't respond to me. I speak and speak, but I don't hear Him. I ask questions, but He doesn't answer me."

What a lesson our daughter was teaching us! We had to explain that God always hears us and that we can learn to listen to Him. With simple examples, we helped her identify God's voice speaking to our spirit. We also taught her that sometimes God responds, but His answer may be "No," or He may require us to wait.

Children will challenge us in everything we believe we know about theology, and they will also show us that what we say about God sometimes doesn't seem logical.

One day when we were driving, Victoria asked us, "How can God live in heaven without falling?" To be honest, it took me several minutes to understand what she was really asking. At her young age, she did not yet know the concept that God is spirit. She pictured Jesus and God with a body like hers. She also knew that in the air, nothing can stay up without wings, so she thought God must constantly be moving to avoid falling! Her interpretation of the phrase "God lives in heaven" made us realize that what is clear and normal to us is not necessarily so for a small child who lacks all the information.

Talking about faith with your children will require your time, dedication, and curiosity.

On a different day, Victoria asked another great question: "How can God live in my heart if He is so big?" Again, we didn't immediately understand what she meant, but eventually, we realized she was comparing the physical size of her chest with what she knew about God. She sang, "My God is so big, so strong, and so mighty, there's nothing my God cannot do." It made no logical sense to her that such a great God could fit or be contained inside her little physical heart. She had every reason to be confused!

Her question showed us something very profound: Telling a child "Jesus lives in your heart" can make God seem like a tiny being that can shrink down to fit inside. We had to explain to Victoria the concept that God lives through His Spirit within us. That His love invades our hearts and that when we say "heart," we don't mean the organ on the left side of the chest that pumps blood. Victoria was right—it's a bit complicated, isn't it?

Talking about faith with your children will require your time, dedication, and curiosity.

One way to know if children are truly understanding concepts is to ask them questions like, "What do you think about what we just read?" or "How would you explain to a friend what we just learned?" At the same time, when questions arise, we must seek honest and clear answers for their inquiries. It won't always be easy to think of a way to make our responses make sense to our kids. At times, we may need to consult pastors or children's ministry leaders for help with explanations. Above all, we must always ask the Holy Spirit to give us grace and the right words to teach our children with clarity and truth.

Also, keep in mind that talking about faith with your children will require you to set aside for good conversations. Our best discussions with Victoria about these topics happened in the car (when we had no electronic devices on) and at bedtime when we shared a Bible reading with her. Make the most of those and other moments to start cultivating faith concepts in your little ones!

CHOOSING THE RIGHT BIBLES AND MATERIAL

Another good piece of advice I can give you regarding teaching the faith is to choose Bibles appropriate for your little ones' ages. Some passages of the Bible are not suitable for them, and that's why these children's Bibles tell the stories in a simple way so that children can enjoy and understand them.

I was a Sunday school teacher from when I was 13 until I was 19. My church had two locations in my city. At the main location, there were many classrooms, so the children were well accommodated according to their ages. At the new location, however, there weren't enough classrooms or teachers, so the age range for a single lesson went from 3 to 10 years old. That's where I developed my skills as a juggler, clown, and who knows how many other things to keep all these little ones calm and "focused" in class!

Both children and adults need the right explanations to understand the heart of the message and what is meant behind what is written.

I remember one of the lessons I had to give–well... let's just say it didn't go all that well. The story was that of Balaam, which we find in Numbers 22. This is the story of a prophet of Israel who receives gifts from a foreign king to curse Israel and avoid having them destroy his kingdom.

Balaam is on his way somewhere, and on part of the road an angel with a drawn sword appears, and the donkey Balaam is riding veers too far off the road to avoid the angel. In doing so, it crushes the prophet's leg. He couldn't see the angel, so he beat the donkey to make it walk down the middle of the road. Then, after several beatings, the donkey spoke and said: "Why are you beating me? I am practically saving your life."

Both children and adults need the right explanations to understand the heart of the message and what is meant behind what is written.

Now, let's be honest: just the fact that in the story the donkey spoke was already alarming. But the worst part is that Balaam argued with the animal! (For my part, I would have run away.) And well... everything was going fine in my class until I got to that point. The look on David's face, an 8-year-old boy, said it all. He simply didn't believe me. But the matter didn't end there. He didn't just look at me incredulously–he started telling everyone out loud: "This teacher really is a liar! How could a donkey talk?" No matter how much I told and retold him that it was written in the Bible and that I hadn't made it up, there was no convincing him, and I wasn't lying. At that moment I realized that not everything we teach from the Bible makes sense to children. And, to be honest, I think that for some of us it doesn't always make sense either. That's why both children and adults need the right explanations to understand the heart of the message and what is meant behind what is written.

BEING VERY CAREFUL WHEN USING THE BIBLE TO CORRECT

It is very common to hear parents, while scolding their children, say: "The Bible says that liars will go to the lake of fire!" Or, even worse, parents telling their children that the Lord will be angry with them if they do something wrong, or that He will get furious and punish them. That is manipulating children into being afraid of doing wrong. However, fear or dread have never been the glue that binds us to God's heart. The only thing that can draw us to God's heart is His love for us and His desire to forgive us and transform us into His image.

Now then, if fear or threats do not work for us adults, they will not be of much use with children either! On the contrary, they will distort God's truth in their lives, as it is very likely that in the future they will not want to be near a punishing God who is watching them even when mom and dad are not around.

In the chapter on parenting and discipline, I gave the example of that time when I wanted to be "very biblical" with my daughter and told her: "Victoria, the Bible says that I have to correct you with a rod, and so I do." As soon as I saw her little face, I realized the mistake I had made. Then she, with a look of disappointment and tears in her eyes, told me: "What? The Bible says that? I don't like the Bible anymore! I can't believe something so cruel is in the Bible!" She loved what the Bible said, but of course she couldn't yet understand the life principle of correction. That principle wasn't for her at that moment! It was for me as a mom! I just had to apply it, not justify my discipline by saying "the Bible says so" as if that gave me more authority. I had heard many parents say that to their children and their children took it very well, so maybe my daughter wasn't ready to hear it... or maybe it's just not right to tell them. I honestly don't know. What I do know is that at that moment she needed to understand that part of my job as a mom was to correct and discipline her because I love her and want the best for her. Then, when she grows up, she will understand that I honored God's Word by correcting her with love, just as God corrects us, His children, with love.

PROVOKING ENCOUNTERS WITH GOD

For our children to learn to encounter God, it is important that we are consistent in having family prayer times.

For our children to learn to encounter God, it is important that we are consistent in having family prayer times. If we do this, they will see that spending time with God is a priority for us.

For our children to learn to encounter God, it is important that we are consistent in having family prayer times.

Also, when our children are still young, these should be F U N moments! They should be times they want to repeat! A good idea is to use children's worship music. Today there is a lot of great children's music available, including songs we adults sing in our worship services but sung by children. They love that! Also, try to have instruments like maracas, drums, tambourines, or other simple items they can play while singing. Dance with them while you praise, and invite them to enjoy this moment of expressing worship to God with all their hearts.

Regarding the Bible story, it doesn't always have to be read; they can watch it on TV or on a tablet. We are members of CBN's Superbook Club, and every month we receive an animated Bible story. Everyone loves it! Sometimes we even end up crying at the end because the story is so well done and so edifying.

Then, during prayer time, model attitudes such as raising your hands to God in gratitude, blowing kisses to God as a sign of love, or kneeling or bowing as a sign of worship. Remember that your children are watching you, and sooner or later they will follow your example.

Sometimes, when we tell our children "Let's pray!" we won't get an enthusiastic response from them. This should not discourage us, nor be a reason to scold them. We will simply do it anyway. And most of the time, they will end up enjoying it!

Be creative when planning this moment of encounter with God. How about bringing them special cookies, or saving something they love to share in that time? My friend, Pastor Rocío Corson, brings her son's favorite gummies to the place where he will spend time with Jesus. She says it's like the carrot in front of the donkey or horse. Rocío wants her son to remember that his favorite treats were eaten with Jesus, just as she enjoys her daily coffee with Jesus every morning. Isn't that a wonderful idea? Without a doubt, "Gummies with Jesus" is a much more fun name for this time than "Devotional Time," right?

In the important task of passing on the faith to your children, you, as a mom, must be determined and intentional. Unlike other responsibilities a mother has, this one is spiritual. On one hand, that makes it more important. On the other, it means you might face spiritual opposition. For this, you must always walk accompanied by the power of the Holy Spirit, and have prayer and God's Word as your greatest weapons. To help you, in the next chapter I will share a prayer guide based on Scriptures that covers many areas of our children's lives.

Chapter 10

PRAYING EFFECTIVELY FOR YOUR CHILD

"And we are confident that he hears us whenever we ask for anything that pleases him. And since we know he hears us when we make our requests, we also know that he will give us what we ask for."
1 John 5:14-15

The Word encourages us to pray because prayer is what connects the supernatural of God with the natural aspects of our lives and those of our children. Maybe you are not a woman who prays long prayers (which, let's be honest, is also very difficult with small children around). With the many responsibilities that we mothers have, often our prayers are limited to giving thanks to God and entrusting the day to Him when we wake up, giving thanks again before eating meals, and perhaps giving thanks once more before finally going to sleep. This is a common prayer practice.

This is one of the most common things, but it is equally true that when someone touches our children, or when our children are in need of a divine intervention in their lives, something happens to our spiritual life, and from our hearts rise the most heart-wrenching and profound prayers heaven has ever heard.

Still, I want to give you some advice: Do not wait until you are in a difficult situation with your little ones to start a life of prayer that opens doors for them, that covers them in every way, and that teaches them how to fight life's battles. Let them see you turn to God in every moment and every circumstance!

OPENING SPIRITUAL EYES

The relationship with God is a personal relationship. Jesus came to open the way so that we can all go to the Father, but the moment when that becomes effective is when each person decides to believe and enter into a relationship with God.

In the Old Testament, we are presented with the story of two men: the prophet Elisha and his servant. The king of Aram, who was at war with the king of Israel, was frustrated because the prophet Elisha was ruining all his attack plans. The prophet warned the king of Israel, on behalf of God, about the places where the Arameans would attack, and so the king of Israel was always prepared. This, of course, greatly annoyed the king of Aram. Because of this, one night, he sent a large army that surrounded the whole city to capture the prophet. When the prophet's servant got up early in the morning, he saw the great army surrounding the city, and in distress, he said to Elisha, "Oh no, my lord! What shall we do?"

At that moment Elisha prayed and asked God to open his servant's eyes... and then he saw the vision of what was happening on a spiritual level: the mountain was full of horses and chariots of fire all around them. Then Elisha asked God to strike the Arameans with blindness, and in this way, the prophet himself led them to the capital, Samaria, to hand them over to the king of Israel. As I see it, prayer is an invitation to know the invisible!

Perhaps you have many questions: How should I pray? Should I pray as it comes to mind, or can I find somewhere some guidance on how to pray? Well, I'll share a secret with you: I have learned that it works best for me to pray using what I know about God—that is, His Word.

God always backs up what He says in His Word.

God always backs up what He says in His Word. So, in prayer, I use His verses, and in this way, I align myself with the truth of what He says, and not with what I may think, wish, or feel for my life and for my children. Remember what we read in the first letter of John: "This is the confidence we have in approaching God: that if we ask anything according to his will, he hears us." (1 John 5:14, NIV)

I can do my best to leave good teachings for my children, I can have an excellent balance between discipline and love, I can invest hours making sure they have a healthy identity, but I cannot reach the place where only God can reveal Himself—inside their being, in their conscience. The Bible teaches us that there is an intimate conversation where only the Spirit of God and the spirit of my child meet. It is where the Spirit convinces my child to be a child of God, and I deny it not for the simple fact that his mom is a daughter of God. As we read in John 16:8–12, the Spirit also convicts my child of sin, because He will rebuke them for wrong actions or thoughts. He convinces them of righteousness so that they will run into the arms of their Savior Jesus Christ. And He convicts them of judgment, so they will know that heaven has already given a verdict in their favor and against the enemy.

Prayer should always be your companion if you truly wish to successfully carry out the raising of your children. Next, I present to you a prayer guide with some Bible verses that can help you cover certain specific topics in your little ones' lives...

PRAYING FOR YOUR CHILD TO HAVE A STRONG FAITH

The first goal in raising our children should be for them to have a personal experience with God. Praying for them to be secure in their salvation is asking God to give them the one gift that will last forever.

Scriptures you can use:

- "For God so loved the world that he gave his one and only Son, that whoever believes in him shall not perish but have eternal life." (John 3:16, NIV)
- "Heavenly Father, I ask that _________ confess with their mouth that Jesus is Lord and believe in their heart that You, God, raised him from the dead, so they may be saved. For it is with your heart that you believe and are justified, and it is with your mouth that you profess your faith and are saved." (Based on Romans 10:9–10, NIV)

PRAYING FOR YOUR CHILD TO LOVE THE WORD OF GOD

Praying for our children to love the Word of God is ensuring them a future of success. There is blessing from God for those who know and put His Word into practice!

Scriptures you can use:

- "Lord, may _________ always study your Word and meditate on it day and night, so that they may be careful to do everything written in it. Then they will be prosperous and successful." (Based on Joshua 1:8, NIV)
- "Jesus, may _________ keep your commands and obey them because they love you. And because he/she loves you, the heavenly Father will love them. Thank you for promising to show yourself to them!" (Based on John 14:21, NLV)

PRAYING FOR YOUR CHILD TO HAVE A NOBLE HEART TOWARD THE VOICE OF GOD

Scriptures you can use:

- "In vain I punished your people; they did not respond to correction." (Jeremiah 2:30, NIV) Lord, I pray that _________ will have a noble heart to heed your correction.
- "Create in _________ a pure heart, O God, and renew a steadfast spirit within them. Do not cast them from your presence or take your Holy Spirit from them. Restore to them the joy of your salvation and grant them a willing spirit, to sustain them." (Based on Psalm 51:10–12, NIV)

PRAYING FOR YOUR CHILD'S SPIRITUAL GIFTS

How wonderful it is to quickly recognize the gifts the Lord has placed in our children's lives! Gifts are important because they have to do with God's purpose for their lives. An advantage of discovering early on the gifts the Lord has given our children is that we can encourage them to use them, telling them how much they bless and help others when they put them into practice. Each child has unique things from God, and we must invite and encourage them to grow and use them to expand His kingdom!

Scriptures you can use:

- "Thank you, Lord, because you have given _________ a spiritual gift to help others." (Based on 1 Corinthians 12:7, NLV)
- "God, from your great variety of spiritual gifts, you have given _________ the gift of _________. I pray that they will use it to serve others well and be a faithful steward of this gift you have given them." (Based on 1 Peter 4:10, NLV)

PRAYING FOR YOUR CHILD TO UNDERSTAND THEIR PURPOSE AS AN AMBASSADOR OF THE KINGDOM OF GOD

We are the light of the world and the salt of the earth; that was the assignment given to us by Jesus Himself. As mothers, we must transmit this conviction to our children. We should tell them: "The world needs someone you were designed to be!" We must also teach them that all our gifts and resources exist for the purpose of being used for the kingdom of God.

Scriptures you can use:

- "Lord, may the light of _________ shine before everyone. May the good deeds that _________ does shine so that people will praise you, our Heavenly Father." (Based on Matthew 5:16, NLV)
- "Lord, may _________ not be ashamed of the gospel, because it is the power of God that brings salvation to everyone who believes: first to the Jew, then to the Gentile." (Romans 1:16, NIV)

PRAYING FOR YOUR CHILD TO HAVE THE FEAR OF THE LORD

Scriptures you can use:

- "Lord, I ask that _________ seek your will in all they do, and that you show them which path to take. May they not be impressed with their own wisdom. Instead, may they fear you and turn away from evil." (Based on Proverbs 3:6–7, NLT)

- "Lord, I pray that my daughter _________ understands that charm is deceptive, and beauty is fleeting; but a woman who fears the Lord is to be praised." (Based on Proverbs 31:30, NIV)

PRAYING FOR WISDOM AND DISCERNMENT FOR YOUR CHILD

Scriptures you can use:

- "If any of you lacks wisdom, you should ask God, who gives generously to all without finding fault, and it will be given to you." (James 1:5, NIV)
- "Lord, I ask that you give _________ complete knowledge of your will and spiritual wisdom and understanding. Then the way they live will always honor and please you, and their lives will produce every kind of good fruit. All the while, _________ will grow as they learn to know you better and better, O God." (Based on Colossians 1:9–10, NLT)

PRAYING FOR YOUR CHILD TO HAVE SELF-CONTROL, DILIGENCE, EXCELLENCE, AND DISCIPLINE

Scriptures you can use:

- "Lord, I ask that my son/daughter _________ present themselves in everything as an example of good works, with integrity, seriousness, and sound speech that cannot be condemned, so that those who oppose them may be ashamed because they have nothing bad to say about them." (Based on Titus 2:7–8, NIV)

- "Lord, I ask that _________ do everything without grumbling or arguing, so that they may become blameless and pure, children of God without fault in a warped and crooked generation. Then they will shine among them like stars in the sky." (Based on Philippians 2:14–15, NIV)
- "Lord, I ask that _________ be skilled in their work. I ask that they be excellent, and serve before kings rather than working for ordinary people." (Based on Proverbs 22:29, NIV)

PRAYING FOR PROTECTION FOR YOUR CHILD

Scriptures you can use:

- "Arise, cry out in the night, as the watches of the night begin; pour out your heart like water in the presence of the Lord. Lift up your hands to him for the lives of your children..." (Lamentations 2:19, NIV)
- "Lord, I ask that my son/daughter _________ take refuge in you and be glad; may they ever sing for joy. Spread your protection over them, that those who love your name may rejoice in you. Bless _________, O Lord, and surround them with your shield." (Based on Psalm 5:11–12, NIV)

PRAYING FOR YOUR CHILD'S HEALTH

Scriptures you can use:

- "Lord, I ask that _________ not be impressed with their own wisdom, but instead fear you and turn away from evil. Then they will have healing for their body and strength for their bones." (Based on Proverbs 3:7–8, NLT)
- "Lord Jesus, I declare that you bore our sins in your body on the cross so that my son/daughter _________ might die

to sins and live for righteousness. By your wounds, Lord Jesus, _________ has been healed." (Based on 1 Peter 2:24, NIV)

- "Lord, your strong right hand is raised in triumph. Your strong right hand has done glorious things! I declare now that my son/daughter _________ will not die but live, and will proclaim what you, Lord, have done." (Based on Psalm 118:16–17, NIV)

PRAYING AGAINST EVERY ACCIDENT

Scriptures you can use:

- "Lord, I ask that my son's/daughter's help come from you. I ask that you will not let their foot slip. Thank you, Lord, because I know you will not slumber or sleep as you watch over my son/daughter _________! Lord, you watch over _________; you keep them from all harm. You watch over their life; you watch over their coming and going both now and forevermore." (Based on Psalm 121, NIV)

PRAYING AGAINST ALL PRESENT EVIL

The world is full of evil and perversion that threatens our children. We truly need God's protection over them!

Scriptures you can use:

- "I declare that you, Lord, are my child _________'s hiding place; you will protect them from trouble and surround them with songs of deliverance." (Based on Psalm 32:7, NIV)

PRAYING FOR SPIRITUAL PROTECTION FOR YOUR CHILD

Scriptures you can use:

- "Lord, I ask that my son/daughter _________ understand that we are not fighting against flesh-and-blood enemies, but against evil rulers and authorities of the unseen world, against mighty powers in this dark world, and against evil spirits in the heavenly places. I ask that they put on all of the spiritual armor you have given, so they will be able to stand firm against all strategies of the devil. I pray, Lord, that _________ will put on every piece of your armor so they will be able to resist the enemy in the time of evil. Then after the battle, my son/daughter _________ will still be standing firm." (Based on Ephesians 6:11–13, NLT)

PRAYING FOR YOUR CHILD'S PROTECTION FROM THE WRONG PEOPLE

There are people who will approach our children, perhaps not with the best intentions. For example, as soon as they enter high school, there will surely be classmates who try to introduce them to drugs or gangs. Even from a young age, they may be victims of jealousy or envy, or simply have friends who do not want what's best for them. As mothers, it is our responsibility to cover them in prayer in these areas too.

Scriptures you can use:

- "The Lord is with me; I will not be afraid. What can mere mortals do to me?" (Psalm 118:6, NIV)
- "I declare that no weapon forged against _________ will prevail, and you will refute every tongue that accuses them. This is the heritage of the servants of the Lord, and

this is their vindication from me, declares the Lord." (Based on Isaiah 54:17, NIV)

PRAYING FOR PROTECTION IN GENERAL

Scriptures you can use:

- "Lord, I ask that my son/daughter _________ live in your shelter and find rest in your shadow. May they declare: 'You are my refuge and my fortress; my God, in whom I trust.' Lord, I ask you to rescue my son/daughter _________ from every trap and protect them from deadly disease. Cover them with your feathers, and let them find refuge under your wings. Your faithful promises are their armor and protection! I ask that _________ not be afraid of the terrors of the night, nor the arrow that flies in the day, nor dread the disease that stalks in darkness, nor the disaster that strikes at midday. I declare that though a thousand fall at their side, though ten thousand are dying around them, these evils will not touch _________. I declare that my son/daughter _________ will see how you punish the wicked. I ask that they make you, Lord, their refuge, and the Most High their shelter, so no evil will conquer them, no plague will come near their home. For you, Lord, will order your angels to protect them wherever they go. They will hold _________ up with their hands so they won't even hurt their foot on a stone. They will trample upon lions and cobras; they will crush fierce lions and serpents under their feet. Lord, I ask that because _________ loves you, you will rescue them. Protect them because they trust in your name. Thank you because I know that when _________ calls on you, Lord, you will answer. You will be with them in trouble. You will rescue and honor them. You will reward them with a long life and give them your salvation." (Based on Psalm 91:1–16, NLT)

PRAYING FOR YOUR CHILD AND THEIR RELATIONSHIP WITH THEIR FRIENDS

Scriptures you can use:

- "As iron sharpens iron, so one person sharpens another." (Proverbs 27:17, NIV)
- "Walk with the wise and become wise, for a companion of fools suffers harm." (Proverbs 13:20, NIV)
- "Lord, please help my child _________ have discernment when choosing friends, and help me as a mother to know how to protect them and teach them to stay away from friendships that will get them into trouble!"

PRAYING FOR YOUR CHILD AND THEIR RELATIONSHIP WITH TEACHERS, PASTORS, AND OTHER AUTHORITIES

Scriptures you can use:

- "Lord, I ask that out of love for you my child _________ submit to all human authority and live an honorable life. May _________ not use their freedom as an excuse to do evil, but live as your servant. I ask that they respect everyone, and love the family of believers. Fear you, O God, and respect the authorities." (Based on 1 Peter 2:13–17, NLT)
- "Heavenly Father, I ask that my son/daughter _________ obey their pastors and submit to them, because they keep watch over their soul as those who must give an account." (Based on Hebrews 13:17, NIV)

PRAYING FOR THE RELATIONSHIP BETWEEN SIBLINGS

Scriptures you can use:

- "How good and pleasant it is when God's people live together in unity! ... For there the Lord bestows his blessing, even life forevermore." (Psalm 133:1,3, NIV)
- "Lord, I ask that you bring that unity into my home!"
- "Lord, I ask that my children be kind and compassionate to one another, forgiving each other, just as in Christ you forgave them." (Based on Ephesians 4:32, NIV)

PRAYING FOR THE VOCATION YOUR CHILD WILL CHOOSE

You may think it's too early to pray for certain matters about your children's future, but the truth is that with your prayer you are paving the way for those plans God has drawn for your children to be fulfilled in His perfect timing for their lives.

When it comes to vocation, you may already notice some inclination in them. Pray asking the Lord to guide them and that from now on they begin to acquire knowledge that will lead them to excellence when they grow up.

Scriptures you can use:

- "Since ancient times no one has heard, no ear has perceived, no eye has seen any God besides you, who acts on behalf of those who wait for him." (Isaiah 64:4, NIV)
- "For the Lord gives wisdom; from his mouth come knowledge and understanding." (Proverbs 2:6, NIV)

PRAYING FOR THEIR FUTURE SPOUSE

I always remember the prayer my mom prayed daily for our future spouses (mine and my siblings'). It was very simple:

- "Lord, I pray for the person you will bring into my children's lives. May it be in your pleasing and perfect time. Lord, put fear and trembling in every person who comes with wrong intentions toward them."

Today I can testify how that prayer guarded me—even against my own will! I remember a guy in college who was very charismatic and attractive. We weren't in the same department, but he was a student leader, and I would often see him in various activities, realizing that I was drawn to him. However, he never dared to say hello. A year later, he had graduated, but I became friends with one of his friends. My friend told me that he actually liked me but never approached me because he was intimidated! Immediately, my mother's prayer echoed in my mind, and I said to myself: "Of course! My mom's prayer scared him away!" I thanked God for that, because His protection kept my life and preserved me for my beloved husband.

Scriptures you can use:

- "He who finds a wife finds what is good and receives favor from the Lord." (Proverbs 18:22, NIV)

- "Lord, I ask that my son _________ receive your favor, and that you choose for him a wife who will truly be a treasure for his life."

- "The Spirit of the Lord will rest on him—the Spirit of wisdom and of understanding, the Spirit of counsel and of might, the Spirit of the knowledge and fear of the Lord." (Isaiah 11:2, NIV)

- "Lord, I ask that my daughter _________ have a husband who has the same Spirit of Christ."

If you want more verses to pray, I recommend the book by Jodie Berndt, *Praying the Scriptures for Your Children*. It not only provides many Bible references that can be useful, but also contains valuable information about each area of prayer.

Chapter 11

FOR SINGLE MOTHERS

"Father of the fatherless and protector of widows is God in his holy habitation."
Psalm 68:5

This chapter is very special to me. Although I am not a single mother, I come from a home where my mother was fully responsible for raising my two brothers and me. At the time of my parents' separation, my older brother was 10 years old, I was eight, and my youngest brother was a year and a half. Today, I can say with certainty that my mother did an excellent job. God's Word says, "By their fruits, you will know them," and we, who are her fruits, are all now fully involved in ministry.

I want to encourage you, Mom, who feels alone in this arduous task, to believe that with the Lord's help, you will do this job very well. In the end, you will be rewarded!

THE LORD IS THE FOUNDATION IN OUR LIVES

The home I was born into was not founded on Christian principles. My father was a successful businessman, handsome and uniquely charismatic. My mother was younger than him, beautiful, and very dedicated to the home and some of the family businesses. After 12 years together, she became aware of my father's infidelity and did not accept the situation.

When she discovered my father's unfaithfulness, she carefully made a plan. She prepared a house that my father had given her and saved money from the rental income from another house he had also given her and from her work in school transportation. One morning, my brother and I left for school from one house... and after school, we were taken to a new one. A house with our things but without our father.

Although we were young, we understood what was happening in our home. In those last months, the situation had been tense, and although Dad and Mom resolved their issues privately, we still knew what was going on.

That afternoon, my mother told us that we now had this new house and that she would make sure it was a place of peace for us.

Even though we understood the strain in our parents' marriage, their separation caused grief—the kind of grief adults and children alike experience in that situation. Between that morning and the afternoon, I had "lost" my father—not because he had died, but because the separation meant we did not see him for several months.

Children pay a high price when adults cannot live with respect and harmony! And situations like ours are even more difficult because one person takes full responsibility for the home when two were called to sustain the family!

I cried for my father for many months. I attended a Catholic school, and during recess, I didn't want to play. Instead, I would go to the chapel to pray and ask for help from this God I only knew about from what school had taught me.

I don't know how the mother's superior found out about this, but one day she waited in the chapel for me. She was an angel to me. Without saying anything, she put me on her lap and prayed with me. I cried and told her how sad I was. She prayed. That was the last day I visited the chapel during recess. I don't know how, but I knew that the Lord was with us and that we were going to be okay.

The mercy of God and His plans are so great that just a few months before my mom decided to separate from my father, her sister-in-law had visited and had shared the Gospel with my mother. When my father learned about my mom's interest in the Lord, he told her she had to choose between God and him.

After the separation, my mom was the sole authority in the home, and she sought a spiritual life for all of us. We started attending prayer groups on Thursdays at a charismatic Catholic church. Soon after that, we joined an Assemblies of God church, which at that time met in a big, beautiful house. That was our spiritual home for many years.

As a family, we knew we were no longer alone. We began to grow in our knowledge of God's Word and make it alive in us. We relied on two Bible verses during that time:

"Father of the fatherless and protector of widows is God in his holy habitation." (Psalm 68:5, NIV)

"I was young and now I am old, yet I have never seen the righteous forsaken or their children begging bread." (Psalm 37:25)

Although my father was alive, we realized that we depended 100% on God. We no longer had my father's physical presence, and for a time, we also lacked his financial support. Because of this, these verses became our reality. If I wanted to tell you everything the Lord did for us—how He healed us, provided for us, instructed us—I would need to write another book!

EVERY CHILD NEEDS A FATHER

No matter what your experience with your husband was, you need a lot of wisdom not to express bitterness, anger, or frustration by speaking badly about him to your children.

My mother was always prudent and never spoke badly about my father. We only knew what was happening because, although they argued in private, there were things we overheard and saw.

I'm not telling you to hide the truth. The truth is important for children to understand—but that doesn't mean there should be constant mentions of your ex's mistakes colored with your emotional pain. It's normal in any conflict to want others to take your side, but you are the guardian of your own heart and, more importantly, of your children's hearts.

When a child has a bad image of their father—whether because of experience or repeated stories—they may struggle to approach God. They may understand that God is almighty and merciful, even good, but it will be hard for them to see Him as their Father. As a result, they might grow up dealing with an orphan spirit, where they feel they must fight for everything they need or want. Another common consequence of having a bad image of their father is struggling with jealousy and envy. A child with a bad or weak relationship with their father will also struggle with identity—how they perceive themselves and, consequently, how they feel about themselves. Deep down, they will likely question whether God loves them as His child as they struggle to understand what a real father is like.

When Jesus Christ came to earth, His purpose in coming, apart from saving us from our sins, was to give us the way to the Father's heart.

When Jesus Christ came to earth, He said of Himself: "I am the way and the truth and the life. No one comes to the Father except through me." (John 14:6, NIV). His purpose in coming, apart from saving us from our sins, was to give us the way to the Father's heart. The Jews marveled and even became angry when they heard Him refer to God as His Father. However, Jesus Himself taught His disciples to speak to God as Father: "Our Father in heaven..."

The good news, then, is that our children's identity and emotional health can be restored when they connect with their Heavenly Father. But you must know that this is only possible when they can forgive any negative action from their father toward them or toward you.

In my personal experience of beginning to replace my absent father with my Heavenly Father, one night, about a year after the separation, missing my dad, I prayed to God like this: "Lord, You say that You call Yourself Father. When I lived with my dad, he was the one who woke me up every morning. I want You to show up in my life as Father, and I want You to be the one to wake me up in the morning just like he used to." After praying, I didn't set my alarm clock. At the exact time I needed to wake up, I clearly heard a voice say to me: "GLORIANA." It was so clear and strong that I woke up immediately. I was amazed and asked myself, "Was that You, Lord?" But right away, I realized it was obviously His answer. Well, of course! Who else could it be?

That day I gave so many thanks to the Lord for answering me! It was so beautiful of God to give me that experience, which truly marked me forever! Never again did I doubt that I have a God who hears my desires and wants to reveal Himself as my Father!

I was only 9 years old when I had this experience. From that moment on, I began to truly enjoy my relationship as a daughter of my Father God. I knew He loved me, cared for me, corrected me... and He still does. With tenderness and firmness, His hand will never turn against me. I am on His radar, He never sleeps, and I am safe in Him.

The Lord's presence as Father also became evident in key moments of my adolescence and youth. Even years later, as a married woman, I was deeply impacted by reading Dr. Meg Meeker's book Strong Fathers, Strong Daughters, which I recommend especially in the chapter on sexuality. Although the book is not written for daughters but for fathers, reading it I discovered how important the presence of a father is in a daughter's life. And the Lord used this book to finish healing some areas in my life that I only understood in that moment, as I read!

Dr. Meeker was for many years the president of the American Association of Psychologists. She has been a counselor for more than 25 years to thousands of women from ages 12 to 24. In this book, she identifies the difference between those girls who had present fathers and those who had absent fathers (or fathers who were present but practiced poor fatherhood).

God speaks as a Father into our lives, pronouncing words of affirmation that heal and restore the soul.

The presence of a good father in the life of a girl or adolescent helps with her self-esteem, the way she communicates with the opposite sex, prevents promiscuity, gives her security in herself, and teaches her about masculine pragmatism (in other words, how to control the drama), among other valuable contributions.

As I examined my life in light of this reality, I remembered some of the feelings I had lived with for many years, my fears, and some negative thoughts I was still battling. And in that moment of crisis and renewed grief for what I had not received from my father, the Holy Spirit reminded me of every verse throughout the Bible where God speaks as a Father into our lives, pronouncing words of affirmation that heal and restore the soul. What a blessed moment of freedom! We truly have a God who is near!

"The Lord is near to all who call on him, to all who call on him in truth." (Psalm 145:18, NIV)

Amen!

GUIDE YOUR CHILDREN IN PRAYER TOWARD MERCY AND TRUTH

From the moment we came to Christ, my mother decided to get serious with the Lord. She established that every night, at 7 p.m., we would have family prayer time. We would first pray Psalm 91, and then each one would have their own time of prayer, including my youngest brother, who at that time was only two years old but still actively participated in prayer. The main prayer requests were for my father to come to know the Lord, along with the specific request of the moment. For almost 8 years we interceded for my father's life. And as we prayed for him, the Lord's mercy toward him filled our hearts, and we understood that part of his wrong behavior was due to not knowing the Lord. Years later, my mom shared the message of the Gospel with my dad, and He opened his heart, surrendering his life to the Lord. But even if that had never happened, the most important thing is that while we prayed for him, the Lord had changed our hearts and the way we saw him.

One time, a single mother asked me: "What if my son's father, being a pastor, abandoned us and formed another family? How do I explain that to my son?" I believe it's the same way. Even if the person had the title of pastor or apostle, the reality is that we ALL need to live in communion with the Lord and with the Holy Spirit so we won't fall into temptation. Evidently, this person was not living in that communion when they made that wrong choice, and that is the explanation you can give to the child if your case is similar to this mother's. Jesus teaches that when we maintain a life of communion with God, we overcome temptation, and that the opposite happens when, in private, we abandon our devotion to God.

Invite your child to pray for their father and to forgive him in prayer, just as we are forgiven.

And in any case, whatever your ex-partner's situation may be, invite your child to pray for their father and to forgive him in prayer, just as we are forgiven. I guarantee that this will help them live without extra burdens in their life.

GUARD YOUR HEART

Single mothers, like every human being, have emotional needs, struggle with feelings of loneliness, and long to share their life with someone else. However, unlike other single women, you are now a mother, and any decision you make to emotionally connect with someone will affect your children either positively or negatively.

You might think: "Well, I also have the right to rebuild my life." Of course you do, but be very careful not to open the doors of your home and your heart too quickly, because you could affect the ones you love most.

Some advice I can give you in this regard is:

Be the first to tell your children

If someone is pursuing you, keep the matter as private as possible until you are sure you can take the relationship to another level, and then tell your children.

Keep in mind that your children most likely only have you. They will feel fear with the arrival of this person, because now they will have to share you. Before, you were only for them. The enemy will also work in their minds to plant lies and scare them. They might think: "Now Mom won't love us like before; we'll be second place." Take some time to speak with them privately about this, even before someone new comes into your life. Assure them of your great love for them, and let them know that no one will ever compete with that love.

SOME QUESTIONS YOU MAY ASK:

WHO IS BEHIND THIS BOOK?

E625 is a team of pastors and servants from different countries, different denominations, different church sizes and styles, that love Christ and the new generations.

WHAT IS E625.COM ABOUT?

e625.com

Our passion is to help families and churches find good materials and resources for discipleship of the new generations and that is why our website serves parents, pastors, teachers, and leaders 365 days a year through www.e625.com with free resources.

WHAT IS PREMIUM SERVICE?

ZONA DE CONTENIDO PREMIUM

In addition to reflections and free short materials, we have a service of lessons, series, research, online books, and audiovisual resources to facilitate your task. Your church can access this service with a monthly subscription that allows all the leaders of a local church to download materials to share as a team and make the necessary copies that they find relevant for the different activities of the congregation or their families.

CAN I EQUIP MYSELF WITH YOUR HELP?

INSTITUTO e6 25

It would be a privilege to help you and with that objective we have our events and our possibilities of formal education. Visit www.e625.com/Eventos to find out about our seminars and go to www.institutoE625.com to learn about the online courses offered by Instituto e6.25

DO YOU WANT CONTINUOUS UPDATES?

Register right now for e625.com updates depending on your field of work: children, preteens, teens, young adults.

LET'S LEARN TOGETHER!